THE POLITICS OF FOOD FOR PEACE

Executive-Legislative Interaction

INSTITUTE OF GOVERNMENT RESEARCH
PUBLICATION SERIES

American Government Studies

1. The Role of Political Parties in Congress: A Bibliography and Research Guide,
   Charles Jones and Randall B. Ripley, 1966. $1.50

2. The Politics of Food for Peace: Executive-Legislative Interaction
   Peter A. Toma, 1967.   Hardbound $3.95

Arizona Government Studies

1. State Budget Preparation in Arizona,
   Paul Kelso, 1964. $1.50

2. Vox Populi: The Battle of 103,
   Robert E. Riggs, 1964. $1.50

3. Politics and Legislation: The Office of Governor in Arizona,
   Roy D. Morey, 1965.   Hardbound $4.00

4. The Movement for Administrative Reorganization in Arizona,
   Robert E. Riggs, 1964. $1.50

Comparative Government Studies

1. Relations of the Profundo Rebels With Their Local Parties,
   Jorgen B. Rasmussen, 1966. $1.50

2. Latin American Politics in the United States,
   Rosendo A. Gomez, 1967. $1.50

International Studies

1. Cold War Diplomacy: The Impact of International Conflicts on
   Diplomatic Communications and Travel,
   Clifton E. Wilson, 1966. $1.50

THE POLITICS OF FOOD FOR PEACE

Executive-Legislative Interaction

By PETER A. TOMA

with the assistance of Frederick A. Schoenfeld

THE INSTITUTE OF GOVERNMENT RESEARCH

American Government Studies
Number 2

THE UNIVERSITY OF ARIZONA PRESS

Tucson, Arizona

THE INSTITUTE OF GOVERNMENT RESEARCH

The University of Arizona

Currin V. Shields
Acting Director

David A. Bingham
Associate Director

Research Specialists

Donald M. Freeman	Rosendo A. Gomez	Charles O. Jones
Conrad Joyner	Paul Kelso	David F. Paulsen, Jr.
Peter A. Toma		Clifton E. Wilson

To

HUBERT H. HUMPHREY

*In recognition of his pioneering efforts to make the
Food for Peace program a lasting success*

Foreword

IN THIS SECOND VOLUME of the American Government series, Professor Peter Toma has analyzed in detail the politics involved in providing food aid for foreign nations. Following an examination of the background of Public Law 480, he focuses on passage of the legislation in 1964. The study is more than a case study of the passage of legislation, for the author has specific questions of broad application which he seeks to answer.

Professor Toma is in the Department of Government at the University of Arizona. He is a frequent contributor to political science journals and is editor of a recent volume, *Basic Issues in International Relations* (Boston: Allyn & Bacon, 1967).

CURRIN V. SHIELDS
Acting Director
Institute of Government Research

Preface

WHY DID THE CONGRESSIONAL attitude toward Food for Peace change in 1964? Public Law 480 had constituted a highly significant portion—approximately 34 percent—of the broad program of foreign aid since 1954. Thus an answer to this question becomes fundamental to understanding the future of food aid in the context of American foreign policy. It is in search of such an answer that this study examines the politics of Food for Peace as they were reflected in Congressional decision-making in 1964.

In that year, notwithstanding either the large government surpluses of agricultural commodities or the worldwide rising food deficit, Congress altered the trend toward gradual expansion of Food for Peace. The program was extended for only two years, in contrast to the three-year extension in 1961. A new executive-legislative committee was established to advise the President on certain aspects of the program. Interest rates were raised on loans to foreign countries under Food for Peace auspices. Congress prohibited further sale of U.S. agricultural surpluses to communist nations and curtailed food aid to nations engaged in aggression against other nations friendly to the United States. These and other restrictive measures were resented and opposed by the executive agencies involved in the implementation of Food for Peace.

Analysis of this situation must bear chiefly on the 1964 extension and amendment of Public Law 480; hence the use of research data has been largely confined to that period. However, the need for projection from 1964 into the near future has made it desirable also to utilize some later research data. The areas studied include domestic and foreign postwar agricultural policy and the decision-making process within Congress and the executive agencies administering Food for Peace. In the process of study, major issues of Congressional debate have been identified, patterns of Congressional voting behavior described, and factors and variables affecting Congressional attitudes toward food aid have been isolated.

I wish to express my gratitude to the many individuals who were kind enough to cooperate and thus contribute in their own way to the completion of this study. Among those individuals are the congressmen and senators who responded to my questionnaire and allotted precious time to interviews; the legislative aides and assistants, in particular John J. Heimburger, who shared observations with me; members of the Food for Peace Research-Map Team, under the directorship of Lawrence W. Witt, who volunteered their views while preparing the research map; and the governmental officers of the Food for Peace program—Herbert Turner, Allen D. Berg, Martin Forman, Frank Barlow and Frank Ellis. I am also grateful to the Department of Government, University of Arizona, for its cooperation; to Jimmye S. Hillman, Head, Department of Agricultural Economics, University of Arizona, for his constructive criticism and able suggestions; to the departmental staff in Agricultural Economics for secretarial assistance, and to the University of Arizona Press, through which publication has been effected.

My greatest debt, however, is to Frederick A. Schoenfeld, a graduate student in the Department of Government at the University of Arizona. His assistance in my research contribution to *A Program of Research on Food for Peace* (January 1966) resulted in two rough drafts utilized in Chapters I and V of the present study. Schoenfeld displayed fortitude in typing my dictation of the entire manuscript. His dedication to this project exceeded the duty of a research assistant and his name has been advanced from the acknowledgments section to the title page in order to reflect accurately his contribution.

PETER A. TOMA

Contents

Tables and Figures

TABLES IN TEXT

TABLES IN APPENDICES

FIGURES IN TEXT

Chapter 1

Agricultural Politics and Policy in the United States

NOWHERE ARE THE PROBLEMS of the affluent society expressed with more clarity than in the agricultural sector of the American economy.[1] On the demand side, the United States has reached a national situation where, by and large, the public has few unsatisfied wants in the matter of food supply. There are minor shifts in the composition of food purchases—from consumption of a high proportion of starches to a high proportion of proteins—but the average consumer is presently in a position to buy all the food that he desires. Consequently, the total demand for farm commodities used for food remains relatively constant and unresponsive to changes in price.

On the supply side, the introduction of machinery and advanced technology has enabled the U.S. farmer to produce an ever-increasing supply of commodities with about the same amount of effort as in the past. The United States Department of Agriculture (USDA) has estimated, for example, that the average farm worker supplied farm products for 6.95 persons in 1900, 10.69 persons in 1940, 15.47 persons in 1950, 19.49 persons in 1955, and 33.25 persons by 1964.[2]

A laissez-faire market would long since have forced a reduction in agricultural output to bring the supply of farm products into harmony with demand. The social mood and values of the American public, however, have tempered the laws of supply and demand in agriculture, with agricultural surpluses as one result.[3] Of the several specific variables operative in this modification,[4] the first is the pastoral history of the United States. In 1790, over 90 per cent of the American public was engaged in agricultural occupations. Although this figure declined to 6.5 per cent in 1964,[5] there still exists a strong empathy for the farmer in large segments of the American public. For example, Paarlberg[6] notes a 1952 voter survey which showed that in addition to the American farm population, *per se,* some 13 per cent of the United States population lived on farms, while another 29 per cent had been

1

farm reared. Thus, more than one-third of the United States population may be considered as directly in sympathy with agricultural problems.

A second variable has been compounded of the belief that food production is the backbone of American progress and a fear of the food shortages that have plagued the rest of the world. These feelings are supported in terms of political behavior by the vast numbers of persons employed in agriculture-related occupations, e.g., processing, packaging, and distribution—wholesale and retail. A serious decline in agricultural production would have its economic effect on all of these sectors.

A third strong factor in modifying the laws of supply and demand in agriculture has been the increased role of the central government. As an example, net realized farm income as a percentage of gross farm income declined from a wartime high in 1946 of 51.2 per cent to 30 per cent in 1964,[7] reflecting the lower prices and higher expenses usually referred to as the "cost-price squeeze."

A final explanatory factor is the strategic location of the agricultural vote with respect to national politics. Although rapidly disappearing through migration out of agriculture, the farm vote is still a matter of concern for national candidates. This concern, coupled with the shrewdness of the American farmer about expressing his economic interests in political terms, constitutes an enormous leverage which has been described by Paarlberg:

> How to win the farm vote? "Farmers vote their pocketbooks," the candidate says, repeating a political cliché. "We've got to come up with a program that will increase farm income, or will give the promise of increasing income." This is the dogma which developed in the 1930's.
>
> "If we can put money into the farmer's pocket, we can win his vote," says the candidate, putting this chain of alleged causation together. "And if we win the farmer's vote, we win the Midwest. If we win the Midwest, we win the election. If we win the election, statesmen will hold office. With statesmen prevailing, the country will be saved." This is the rationale that pacifies the conscience. So the stick is supposed to beat the dog, the dog bite the pig, the pig jump over the stile, and all get safely home.[8]

To understand specific agricultural policies, a brief overview is desirable of the politics which produced them. Since agricultural policy is to a great extent determined by Congress, legislative voting patterns provide a reliable index to policy formation.[9]

CONGRESSIONAL VOTING BLOCS

The postwar years have been marked by significant patterns of Congressional voting behavior. Although not conforming absolutely to these patterns, the voting behavior of the Congress has been consistent enough to warrant discussion of voting blocs representing domestic agriculture. Since such blocs are not monolithic. Within each one there may be different reasons for the like voting behavior of diverse groups.

One such bloc of congressmen (bloc 1) has generally voted in favor of high price supports, a high level of assistance to agriculture in general, and production controls. This bloc has been composed of four groups of Senators and Representatives, the first of which is a majority of Western and Southern Democrats. The positions of these congressmen may be explained as a function of the heavy concentrations of farmers in their constituencies; the incidence of farmers in the constituencies of Southern congressmen is higher than anywhere else in the nation. Many farmers in the West and especially in the South are in a below-average income group and, if they are to remain in farming, need the sort of assistance provided by high price supports and production controls. Furthermore, in the South the importance of agriculture to the rest of the economy is relatively high, and other segments of the electorate are interested in the situation of the farmer. (Since the late 1950's, this importance has diminished somewhat with the entrance of the South into the mainstream of contemporary American society and the vast migration out of agriculture; nevertheless, it remains a strong factor.)

Support from the Plains

A second support group in bloc 1 has been composed of Republican congressmen from the Plains area. Their alignment in favor of government support for agriculture may be explained by the fact that wheat is the major crop grown on the Plains. Since the demand for wheat in the United States is generally unresponsive to price changes, constituency pressure on congressmen from these areas has favored high price supports and strict production controls. A third group is composed of Lake States Republican congressmen with heavy concentrations of small farmers in their constituencies who need price guarantees to maintain profits. The fourth and final group is composed of those Corn Belt Republican Representatives coming from small-farm districts where the bulk of the corn crop is sold for cash rather than for feed.

Another Congressional bloc (bloc 2) is composed of congressmen who usually have voted in favor of low government supports for agriculture (and in extreme cases, for termination of all government support programs) and who have favored minimal or nonexistent production controls. This bloc also is composed of four groups, the first consisting of Republican congressmen from urban or suburban areas. Their opposition to government programs may be explained as a combination of party ideology and fear that high supports may raise the cost of food.

A second group in bloc 2 is composed of congressmen from feed deficit areas—especially Republicans from the Northeast where there is a heavy concentration of dairy, poultry, and egg production. The apparent reason for their opposition to government maintenance of agricultural prices is the fact that farmers in these areas buy most of their feed from the Corn Belt. Congressmen from these areas have voted against price supports, fearing that these would increase the prices of feeds in their constituencies. Democratic congressmen from areas with feed deficit problems—Maryland, Florida and Virginia—have opposed price supports for similar reasons. Lake States congressmen do not fit into this group because there the farmers grow most of their own feed.

Opposition from the West

Republicans representing the cattle areas of the West, the Mountain States and the Western Plains especially, are a third group that has opposed price supports. The voting behavior of these congressmen may be partly attributed to the "cheap-feed" motive; an additional factor is that the most influential voters in these areas are big cattle farmers. As such, they oppose price supports and contribute to the election of congressmen who oppose supports and controls on ideological principle.

The Corn Belt congressmen previously mentioned constitute a fourth group which generally opposes supports and controls. Excepting congressmen from areas where the crops are sold for cash, these Republican legislators are elected by farmers fearful of a corn price rise followed by a meat price rise, a reduction in meat sales and consequently in the demand for corn. They are also somewhat apprehensive that a higher price-scale might make corn into a competitive substitute crop for farmers of commodities such as cotton and wheat.

The third and final voting bloc is composed of the Democratic congressmen from urban areas who, because of voting inconsistency, have tended to hold the balance of power in the formation of agricultural policy. On some occasions, they have defended high price supports and production controls on ideological principles or party unity demand. At other times, however, they have voted against such programs on the grounds of maintaining lower food prices for their urban constituents. Over the last twenty years, however, they have voted most often in favor of government intervention.

POLITICAL PARTIES AND FARM GROUPS

The ideologies of the two major political parties have been a vital aspect of agricultural politics in the postwar period. The Democrats generally have favored high price supports. In their legislative requests, Presidents Kennedy and Johnson, as a general principle, have asked for high supports as Truman did subsequent to the defeat of the Brannan Plan in 1949. The majority of the Republicans, on the other hand, have supported a reduction in the level of federal support for agriculture. Many urban Republicans have gone so far as to call for conversion of agriculture into a free-market economy. Some farm-area Republicans, however, have favored government assistance. Such intra-party differences have been resolved at the national level by subscribing to flexible scales of price supports, generally lower than those favored by the Democrats, and less stringent production controls than those supported by Democrats. This was the position of the Eisenhower Administration from 1953-1961.

These stands on the farm problem have largely conformed to and perhaps resulted from the broad ideological positions of the parties— the Republican advocacy of free enterprise and a restricted economic role for the federal government, and the Democratic tendency (since the New Deal) toward economic activism, managed economy, and greater federal responsibility for public welfare. Lest this discussion be interpreted as drawing too clear a distinction between party positions, one is reminded of Paarlberg's "law of agricultural politics": "On any given issue, the major political parties will tend to take positions which are as much alike as possible, yet being distinguishably different."[10] At the national level, differences are of degree, not of kind.

Influence of interest groups

The agricultural interest groups have been another major force shaping political events relevant to postwar farm policy.[11] These numerous and vocal organizations are typified by three national groups having the most impact on farm legislation. The largest of these is the American Farm Bureau Federation, in 1964 claiming a membership of some 1.6 million farm families—mostly from the Midwest—the Corn Belt especially—and from the South. Party affiliation of Bureau members is predominantly Republican in the Midwest and Democratic in the South. Since the 1940's, the Bureau has moved steadily in the direction of favoring a free market for agriculture. While still favoring price supports, it insists that these should do no more than alleviate major price fluctuations. The second major interest group, predominantly Democratic, is the National Farmers Union with only 250,000 families in its membership—mostly in Oklahoma, Montana, Colorado, Utah, Wisconsin, Minnesota, the Dakotas, and Nebraska. In direct opposition to the Farm Bureau, the Farmers Union has generally taken a position in favor of strong governmental assistance to the farmer, stringent production controls, rigid, high-level price supports, and direct cash subsidies to farmers. Such policies reflect the personal attitudes of marginal farmers who make up a large part of the Farmers Union membership.

A third organization of major importance is the National Grange, which claims some 860,000 members. The Grange is strongest in Ohio, Pennsylvania, the Northeast, and the Northwest. While generally favoring high supports and strict production controls in the postwar period, its position has not been nearly as strong in this regard as that of the Farmers Union. In many respects the Grange may be thought of as middle of the road, with the Farm Bureau and the Farmers Union at the extremes of a conservative-liberal continuum.

AGRICULTURAL POLICY AND THE SURPLUS PROBLEM

How have such factors and variables influenced United States agricultural policy? The impact of the politics of agriculture upon governmental policy may be observed at two levels. On the one hand, the general concern of Congress with problems of the farmer has discouraged strong action to adjust agricultural production to the postwar demand for farm products. On the other hand, the influence of agricultural interests continued to shape agricultural policy even after the Congress was finally forced to attempt such adjustments. Both have contributed to the vast government-owned holdings of agricultural commodities which have characterized the postwar period.

The mobilization of agriculture for the Second World War has a direct bearing on the subsequent surplus problem. By 1942, New Deal efforts to reduce the supply of farm produce and therefore to stabilize (and raise) farm incomes had begun to be effective. Thus, when the burden of supplying food for our wartime allies fell upon the United States, it became necessary to stimulate agricultural production, and this stimulus took the form of guaranteed high prices for agricultural commodities. The farmers responded with record crops. Guaranteed prices continued for two years after the war as a result of the foresight of agricultural planners who before the war had realized the disastrous effects of a suddenly reduced demand for agricultural commodities. By 1948 and the end of the European Recovery Period, the demand had dropped sharply, and legislation was enacted prior to the 1948 election to schedule reduction of price supports. This reduction had the support of many Republican congressmen.

Price supports reinstated

In many ways the 1948 election was responsible for the surpluses of the 1950's and early 1960's, since congressmen of both parties attributed the Republican loss of key Midwestern states to the party's price support policy. Although this belief was branded as a mistake,[12] the myth resulted in the new Democratic Congress enacting 1948 legislation to reinstate wartime price supports. The increased demand for food created by the Korean War postponed for a time the inevitable consequences of keeping prices artificially high by government action.

With the end of the Korean conflict in 1953, it soon became apparent that firm action was going to be necessary with respect to agriculture. High price supports stimulated continued high farm output. This, coupled with the government's inability to sell the products that it was forced to buy, and the generally permissive situation concerning regulation of agricultural acreage, resulted in massive government holdings. Not only was the American sense of economic efficiency affronted, but the general public objected to being forced to subsidize agriculture for "useless" production.

Since 1954, there has been a concentrated attack on the problem of agricultural surpluses. It should be noted, however, that this attack has been within the confines of existing agricultural policies. The success of this effort is best expressed in terms of the four tools of agricultural policy: (1) price supports, (2) production controls, (3) surplus disposal programs, and (4) governmental agricultural assistance programs which help the farmer to increase output. All four of these programs affect agricultural surpluses. Efforts under one program to reduce surplus stocks, however, may be canceled out by the results of another.[13]

Perhaps price supports are the most generally understood of the four programs.

Under price supports the government stood ready to take off the market at a given price (the support price) all supplies of specific crops. This tended to maintain the market price at about the level of the support price. The price support was fixed by Congress or by the Secretary of Agriculture within limits set by Congress.[14]

Central to the notion of price supports is the concept of parity,[15] which here meant a method of determining "fair" economic returns for agricultural output. As has been noted earlier, price supports were maintained until 1954 at the high wartime level of 90 percent of parity. Under the Eisenhower Administration, there was a steady reduction of price support levels. In 1961, the Kennedy Administration briefly raised the levels in the effort to improve the income of the small farmer, and since that time, support levels have been forced downward. Table 1.1 reflects these general trends in terms of specific support levels for selected commodities. "Basic" crops are those commodities felt to be essential to the American economy; "nonbasics" are commodities for which Congress has specified price supports as mandatory. In the first two categories, the mandatory nature of the support stems from Congressional directive. Prior to 1954, support at 90 percent of parity was specified. Since 1954, however, Congress has largely specified a range, e.g., 65 to 90 percent of parity, within which the Secretary of Agriculture has discretion to fix the specific support level on the basis of surplus conditions. With respect to "other" commodities, the Secretary of Agriculture has the authority under 1938 legislation to support any commodity at 0 to 90 percent of parity as he sees fit; the commodities in Table 1.1 under this category represent the exercise of such discretion.

Use of production control

A second government policy which has been brought to bear on the postwar farm problem is production control. It has been used in two basic forms—acreage allotments and marketing quotas—to reduce agricultural production. Both the allotment and the quota are based on a reduction of the number of acres that a farmer can use for a

TABLE 1.1

Price supports for major commodities, 1945-64

Figures below show percentages of parity, rounded to nearest full unit, at which farm products were supported from 1945-64. Actual support levels *offered* are shown. Commodites are arranged according to 1964 classification as basic (supports mandatory), mandatory non-basic (supports mandatory) or other (supports optional in discretion of Secretary of Agriculture). Supports were available for certain types of extra-long-staple cotton before 1953, but uniform figures are not available. Elsewhere, a dash means no supports were available that year.

	1945	1946	1947	1948	1949	1950	1951	1952	1953	1954
Basic										
Corn	90	90	90	90	90	90	90	90	90	90
Upland cotton	93	93	93	93	90	90	90	90	90	90
Extra-long-staple cotton	—	—	—	—	—	—	—	—	105	91
Peanuts	90	90	90	90	90	90	88	90	90	90
Rice	90	90	90	90	90	90	90	90	91	91
Wheat	90	90	90	90	90	90	90	90	91	90
Burley tobacco	90	90	90	90	90	90	90	91	91	91
Flue-cured tobacco	90	90	90	90	90	90	90	91	92	90
Mandatory non-basics										
Butterfat*	90	90	90	90	90	86	90	90	90	75
Mfg. Milk*	90	90	90	90	90	79	87	90	90	75

* 1960 prices before special legislation.

Source: *Congress and the Nation*, p. 672.

TABLE 1.1 (continued)

	1945	1946	1947	1948	1949	1950	1951	1952	1953	1954
Mandatory non-basics										
Honey**	—	—	—	—	—	60	60	70	70	70
Mohair	—	—	—	—	—	74	74	75	80	83
Tung Nuts	137	—	—	—	60	60	60	62	65	60
Wool	132	129	101	94	94	90	90	90	90	90
Barley	75	75	73	75	72	75	75	80	85	85
Sorghum grain	79	80	76	77	70	65	75	80	85	85
Oats	70	74	69	70	70	75	75	80	85	85
Rye	60	—	—	72	72	75	75	80	85	85
Other										
Dry edible beans	90	90	90	90	80	75	75	85	87	80
Cottonseed	136	—	—	—	90	73	90	90	75	75
Flaxseed	96	115	160	143	90	60	60	80	80	70
Soybeans	123	104	90	90	90	80	90	90	90	80
Chickens	90	90	90	90	90	—	—	—	—	—
Eggs	90	90	90	90	90	75	—	—	—	—
Hogs	98	90	90	90	90	—	—	—	—	—
Dry smooth peas	102	95	90	90	60	—	—	—	—	—
Potatoes	90	90	90	90	60	60	—	—	—	—
Sweet potatoes	90	90	90	90	80	—	—	—	—	—
Turkeys	90	90	90	90	90	—	—	—	—	—
Crude Pine Gum	—	—	—	—	—	—	90	90	90	90

** Figure for 1947 not available.

TABLE 1.1 (continued)

	1955	1956	1957	1958	1959	1960	1961	1962	1963	1964
Basic										
Corn	87	84	77	77	66	65	74	74	79	80
Upland cotton	90	83	78	81	80	75	82	82	79	80
Extra-long-staple cotton	76	75	75	65	65	65	65	65	70	66
Peanuts	90	86	81	81	75	79	86	82	80	79
Rice	86	83	82	75	75	75	79	76	73	74
Wheat	83	83	80	75	77	75	76	83	83	80
Burley tobacco	91	90	90	90	90	†	†	†	†	†
Flue-cured tobacco	91	90	90	90	90	†	†	†	†	†
Mandatory non-basics										
Butterfat*	76	81	79	75	77	76	81	75	75	75
Mfg. Milk*	80	84	82	75	77	76	83	75	75	75
Honey**	70	70	70	70	60	60	75	75	67	65
Mohair	91	92	86	82	75	74	72	70	72	68
Tung Nuts	60	65	65	65	65	66	82	81	73	73
Wool	106	106	101	95	88	86	84	83	84	80
Barley	70	76	70	70	60	61	74	74	76	77
Sorghum grain	70	76	70	70	60	61	78	78	79	80
Oats	70	76	70	70	60	60	74	74	77	77
Rye	70	76	70	70	60	69	69	69	73	75

† Tobacco support system changed by 1960 law; supports in 1960-61 were at same dollars and cents level as 1959: 55.5 cents for flue-cured, 57.2 cents for burley. Burley was supported at 57.8 cents in 1962, 58.3 cents in 1963, and 58.9 cents in 1964. Flue-cured was supported at 56.1 cents in 1962, 56.6 cents in 1963, and 57.2 cents in 1964.

TABLE 1.1 (*continued*)

	1955	1956	1957	1958	1959	1960	1961	1962	1963	1964
Other										
Dry edible beans	70	70	68	68	60	60	70	70	67	68
Cottonseed	65	70	65	65	57	57	78	76	70	70
Flaxseed	65	70	65	65	60	62	74	76	75	76
Soybeans	70	75	70	70	64	64	79	78	75	74
Chickens	—	—	—	—	—	—	—	—	—	—
Eggs	—	—	—	—	—	—	—	—	—	—
Hogs	—	—	—	—	—	—	—	—	—	—
Dry smooth peas	—	—	—	—	—	—	—	—	—	—
Potatoes	—	—	—	—	—	—	—	—	—	—
Sweet potatoes	—	—	—	—	—	—	—	—	—	—
Turkeys	—	—	—	—	—	—	77	88	—	—
Crude Pine Gum	90	90	90	90	89	84	—	—	84	84

given crop. Within the specified acreage, he can produce as much as he desires or is able. The two programs differ in the nature of the sanctions for noncompliance with government specifications. In the case of the farmer who exceeds the allotment, the government revokes his eligibility for payments under the price support programs. As an enforcement procedure, this device has not proven successful, since price supports effectively maintain the market price at about the level of the support. In the absence, therefore, of massive noncompliance, the individual farmer can obtain more profit by exceeding allotments and selling his produce on the open market. In the case of the quota, however, noncompliance can subject the farmer to fine and civil penalty in addition to loss of eligibility for price support programs. Due to the enormous political leverage that the farmer has, quotas have been imposed only when the supply situation has made them essential. Table 1.2 indicates the nature of allotment and quota programs which the government has imposed in recent years on the most significant agricultural commodities. During the Second World War and the European Recovery Period, there were production controls in effect only on tobacco. Following their brief introduction in 1950 for all basic commodities (except extra long staple cotton), controls on everything but peanuts and tobacco were removed again in response to the agricultural demand created by the Korean War.

With the general overhaul of farm legislation in 1954, production controls were reestablished for all basics. In many instances quotas have been specified. Since 1954, the picture of production control has been one of steadily reduced allotments or quotas in an effort to bring the surplus situation under control. With the exception of wheat farmers in referendum rejecting allotments in 1963, farmers generally have voted to retain high supports by reducing production acreage.

A third policy designed to alleviate the surplus problem has involved programs for disposal of surplus.[16] In general terms, there have been two types of such legislation. On the one hand are programs designed to reduce stocks of commodities stored by the government as a result of price support operations. Authorized under this type are sales for dollars and export subsidies, donations of food to needy persons in the United States and foreign countries, and the barter of agricultural commodities for materials needed either by the various federal agencies or the national stockpiles. The other type of program has been designed to remove surpluses before they have been acquired by the government under support operations or, in some instances, to dispose of nonsupported surpluses. Under a 1935 provision,

TABLE 1.2

Acreage allotments for basic commodities, 1945-64

Allotments in effect for basics are indicated in thousands of acres below. Blank space means allotments not in effect. "M" indicates marketing quotas also in effect. Asterisk (*) indicates allotments were terminated during year.

	Wheat	Corn	Rice	Peanuts	Upland Cotton	X-long Staple	Burley Tobacco	Flue-cured Tobacco
1945							609M	1,118M
1946							557M	1,257M
1947							469M	1,247M
1948				2,359M*			463M	908M
1949				2,629M			468M	959M
1950	72,776	46,247	1,593	2,200M	21,000M		418M	969M
1951	72,785*		1,868*	1,889M			472M	1,119M
1952				1,706M			475M	1,127M
1953				1,678M			433M	1,045M
1954	62,809M	46,996	1,928M	1,610M	21,379M	41M	399M	1,053M
1955	55,802M	49,843	1,653M	1,650M	18,113M	46M	309M	1,007M
1956	56,226M	43,281	1,653M	1,611M	17,391M	45M	309M	888M
1957	55,000M	37,289	1,653M	1,612M	17,585M	89M	309M	711M
1958	55,000M	38,818	1,653M	1,612M	17,554M	83M	309M	712M
1959	55,000M		1,653M	1,612M	17,327M	71M	309M	713M
1960	55,000M		1,653M	1,612M	17,533M	65M	309M	713M
1961	55,000M		1,653M	1,612M	18,458M	64M	329M	714M
1962	49,603M**		1,818M	1,610M	18,102M	100M	349M	745M
1963	55,000M		1,818M	1,610M	16,250M	150M	349M	708M
1964	49,500M		1,818M	1,613M	16,200M	113M	316M	638M

** Temporary mandatory cutback in effect.

SOURCE: Agriculture Department.

an amount equal to 30 percent of all customs receipts has been appropriated to the Secretary of Agriculture for purposes including market purchase of commodities and their donation to welfare institutions. In 1946, provision was made for the school lunch program, under which direct cash grants were made to states so that food could be purchased for nonprofit lunches at schools; in 1954, a similar milk program was enacted. Finally, in 1964, a Food Stamp Plan was made permanent. Under its provisions, stamps were sold to needy persons who could, in turn, redeem them at certain stores for food worth more than the stamps had cost.

One other program—under which surpluses are sold or donated to foreign countries—cuts across both other types of surplus disposal programs. Authorized by the Agricultural Trade Development and Assistance Act of 1954, the program is commonly referred to as Public Law 480. Under its provisions, commodities from either government stocks or other surplus holdings may be donated for certain purposes or sold at concessional prices. As Public Law 480 forms the legislative base of Food for Peace, an extended treatment of it will follow in the next chapter.

The fourth government policy tool relates to a series of provisions for government assistance to the individual American farmer—to make him more efficient in production. The two most significant programs of this type can be classified as research programs (providing also for dissemination of knowledge thus acquired) and various conservation programs designed to increase and maintain the productivity of agricultural land.

Clearly, American agricultural policy is complex, and any brief treatment tends toward oversimplification. Table 1.3 indicates the variety of specific programs in the general policy areas outlined. It indicates also the relative magnitude of expenditure for such programs.

Appraisal of surplus situation

What is the surplus situation as a result of the application of these four separate policy tools? One way to answer this question is to examine the stocks of agricultural commodities acquired by the Commodity Credit Corporation (CCC) under price support operations.[17] Since legislation enacted in 1954 went into effect in 1956, the government, to a great extent, has been able to hold the line on surpluses at about $7 billion worth of commodities. Figure 1.1 reveals the magnitude and composition of CCC holdings of agricultural commodities.

TABLE 1.3

Agriculture expenditures for all programs—1957-66

(Note—Amounts reported are based on expenditures for the Department of Agriculture as shown in the Budget. Figures are adjusted for comparability with the appropriation structure in the 1966 Budget.)

(Millions of Dollars in Each Fiscal Year)

	1957	1958	1959	1960	1961	1962	1963	1964	Estimated 1965	Estimated 1966
General activities										
Agricultural Research Service:										
Salaries and expenses	109.2	120.0	139.9	133.0	148.1	158.0	171.5	190.5	219.5	243.5
Salaries and expenses (special foreign currency program)	—	—	—	—	1.6	3.1	4.2	4.8	6.8	8.3
Construction of facilities	1.1	1.0	3.7	8.2	3.6	2.1	4.1	1.7	1.0	0.4
Cooperative State Research Service (principally payments to States)	29.4	30.9	32.0	31.9	33.0	36.0	38.0	41.7	50.7	53.4
Extension Service (principally payments to States)	51.8	58.7	63.1	63.6	67.2	70.2	74.6	79.3	85.3	86.4
Farmer Cooperative Service	0.7	0.9	0.9	0.9	1.0	1.0	1.0	1.1	1.1	1.2
Soil Conservation Service:										
Conservation operations	65.8	71.6	84.3	79.2	86.8	88.9	92.9	95.9	103.6	104.0
Watershed planning	3.9	4.5	4.7	4.6	5.0	5.4	5.6	5.1	5.4	5.7
Watershed protection	7.4	9.3	14.9	22.4	27.6	34.2	47.4	57.6	59.6	64.8
Flood prevention	10.6	12.1	15.6	16.8	17.5	19.4	26.5	22.4	25.3	25.7
Great Plains conservation program	—	1.6	5.4	7.9	8.6	9.0	9.7	11.9	13.2	14.4
Resource conservation and development	—	—	—	—	—	—	—	0.3	1.8	3.7

TABLE 1.3 (continued)

	1957	1958	1959	1960	1961	1962	1963	1964	Estimated 1965	Estimated 1966
Economic Research Service	6.8	7.3	7.6	7.6	7.9	8.3	8.8	9.4	10.5	11.3
Statistical Reporting Service	5.2	5.8	6.3	6.3	7.5	8.7	9.4	10.5	11.9	14.3
Agricultural Marketing Service:										
Marketing services	13.1	14.9	24.1	23.7	29.7	31.0	35.4	38.3	39.5	41.4
Payments to States and possessions	1.2	1.2	1.2	1.2	1.2	1.3	1.4	1.5	1.5	1.5
Special milk program (financed by CCC prior to fiscal year 1963)	—	—	—	—	—	—	95.3	97.3	103.0	100.0
School lunch program	98.9	99.7	143.5	152.6	154.1	168.8	169.3	180.3	190.9	202.0
Food stamp program (financed under removal of surplus agricultural commodities in fiscal years 1961-1964)	—	—	—	—	—	—	—	—	59.6	99.6
Foreign Agricultural Service:										
Salaries and expenses	4.8	5.4	6.0	5.6	6.5	8.2	11.8	16.7	19.9	20.5
Salaries and expenses (special foreign currency program)	—	—	—	—	6.3	6.7	4.6	3.1	2.8	2.5
Commodity Exchange Authority	0.8	0.8	0.9	0.9	1.0	1.0	1.0	1.1	1.2	1.2
Agricultural Stabilization and Conservation Service:										
Expenses, Agricultural Stabilization and Conservation Service	132.2	120.3	101.1	86.7	83.3	95.6	98.4	114.5	111.6	136.7
Sugar Act program	65.2	67.5	65.1	71.7	69.7	78.0	76.9	87.1	103.0	95.0

TABLE 1.3 (*continued*)

	1957	1958	1959	1960	1961	1962	1963	1964	Estimated 1965	Estimated 1966
Agricultural conservation program	236.9	188.2	213.0	209.3	220.2	227.0	212.6	217.0	232.0	226.1
Indemnity payments to dairy producers	—	—	—	—	—	—	—	—	8.8	—
Conservation reserve program	—	97.0	158.9	305.4	350.8	332.7	305.4	289.9	197.0	152.2
Acreage reserve program	309.9	585.3	653.8	0.2	—	—	—	—	—	—
Cropland conversion program	—	—	—	—	—	—	4.0	7.1	14.2	8.4
Rural Community Development Service	—	—	—	—	—	—	0.1	0.1	0.1	0.7
Office of the Inspector General	4.8	6.0	6.5	6.7	7.6	8.0	8.9	9.5	9.7	10.9
Office of the General Counsel	2.6	2.7	3.1	2.9	3.2	3.3	3.5	3.8	4.1	4.2
Office of Information	1.6	1.4	1.5	1.3	1.5	1.5	1.6	1.4	1.7	1.7
National Agricultural Library	0.7	0.6	0.7	0.7	0.8	0.9	1.1	1.4	1.9	3.9
Office of Management Services	1.5	1.6	1.7	1.8	2.1	2.1	2.4	2.5	2.2	2.6
General Administration	2.1	2.3	2.6	2.5	2.7	2.7	3.0	3.4	3.5	3.9
Forest Service:										
Forest protection and utilization	83.3	95.6	116.5	129.9	156.1	189.8	197.8	204.4	217.5	202.9
Forest roads and trails	26.5	20.9	35.5	27.8	31.1	32.3	39.4	58.9	84.9	78.7
Access roads	—	—	—	—	1.8	0.2	0.8	1.6	1.4	—
Acquisition of lands for national forests	0.2	0.3	0.6	0.1	0.1	0.3	0.8	1.0	1.5	0.1
Acquisition of lands, Klamath Indians	—	—	—	—	68.7	—	—	—	—	—
Assistance to States for tree planting	—	0.1	0.4	—	—	0.5	1.2	1.0	1.0	1.0

TABLE 1.3 (continued)

	1957	1958	1959	1960	1961	1962	1963	1964	Estimated 1965	Estimated 1966
Other (principally interfund transactions)	-2.6	-5.0	-2.8	-3.4	-3.3	-2.9	-2.7	-4.7	-1.1	-0.1
Total, General Activities	1,275.6	1,630.5	1,912.3	1,410.0	1,610.6	1,633.3	1,767.7	1,870.4	2,009.3	2,034.7
Credit agencies										
Rural Electrification Administration:										
Electrification and telephone loans	258.9	288.2	305.0	321.0	291.5	293.0	331.7	330.2	355.0	365.0
Salaries and expenses	8.1	8.6	9.8	9.3	9.8	9.8	10.3	11.2	11.8	11.9
Farmers Home Administration:										
Rural housing grants and loans	20.9	30.2	60.5	43.3	57.7	106.2	184.2	130.6	146.1	41.9
Rural housing for the elderly fund	—	—	—	—	—	—	—	0.1	9.0	4.6
Rural housing for domestic farm labor	—	—	—	—	—	—	—	—	—	5.0
Real estate and operating loans[a]	211.0	223.1	218.5	229.1	267.2	71.6	55.0	56.1	47.6	17.7
Emergency credit revolving fund	9.7	-4.7	-31.1	-17.8	1.5	35.4	7.4	-9.1	17.7	5.9
Agriculture credit insurance fund	6.9	-5.1	26.2	6.8	-6.1	-7.2	13.5	42.5	-15.3	-11.8
Rural renewal	—	—	—	—	—	—	—	0.1	1.8	2.8
Salaries and expenses	26.9	28.1	31.6	30.0	31.9	33.4	34.9	38.3	41.0	44.6
Total, Credit Agencies	542.4	568.4	620.5	621.7	653.5	542.2	637.0	599.9	614.6	487.5

a Reduced expenditures beginning with fiscal year 1962 reflect establishment of a direct loan account in the year pursuant to Section 338(c) of the Consolidated Farmers Home Administration Act of 1961. Under this Act, collections of principal and interest on loans are deposited into the direct loan account, thereby reducing expenditures.

TABLE 1.3 (continued)

	1957	1958	1959	1960	1961	1962	1963	1964	Estimated 1965	Estimated 1966
Corporations (net)										
Federal Crop Insurance Corporation:										
Operating and administrative expenses	6.1	6.3	6.3	6.3	6.5	6.0	6.7	7.0	7.5	8.5
Federal Crop Insurance Corporation fund	7.4	-4.9	-14.5	-2.4	-6.8	1.1	7.7	-0.8	-0.4	1.2
Commodity Credit Corporation:										
Price-support and related programs[b]	1,086.8	986.8	2,774.9	1,480.2	1,330.6	2,051.5	3,117.4	3,175.3	2,292.6	1,863.7
Special milk program	57.0	66.7	74.7	81.2	87.0	91.7	-1.6	-0.4	—	—
Special activities financed from CCC funds:										
Loans to Secretary of Agriculture for conservation purposes	-13.0	21.5	7.0	-0.3	1.0	11.9	7.9	-0.6	—	—
Military housing (Public Law 161, 84th Congress, barter and exchange)	0.5	11.1	31.5	6.0	-2.0	-1.9	-1.6	-3.0	-2.4	-2.0
National Wool Act	61.3	57.2	20.0	92.7	60.9	65.3	63.2	72.9	31.8	38.5
Research to reduce surplus commodities	—	—	—	—	—	—	—	—	6.8	5.9
Other	—	-0.5	0.4	0.2	-2.5	2.3	0.2	-11.8	-3.9	-0.6
Total, Commodity Credit Corporation	1,192.6	1,142.8	2,908.5	1,660.0	1,475.0	2,220.8	3,185.4	3,232.4	2,324.9	1,905.5

b Net, after sales from inventories.

TABLE 1.3 (continued)

	1957	1958	1959	1960	1961	1962	1963	1964	Estimated 1965	Estimated 1966
Foreign Assistance Programs:										
Public Law 480:										
Sale of surplus agricultural commodities for foreign currencies[c]	1,337.9	1,073.2	1,022.0	1,232.0	1,454.7	1,454.8	1,483.0	1,415.3	1,246.7	1,140.0
Commodities disposed of for emergency famine relief to friendly peoples	124.9	121.4	97.9	95.5	198.6	241.9	215.6	228.2	210.5	305.6
Long-term supply contracts	—	—	—	—	—	29.0	80.2	60.5	204.3	215.5
International Wheat Agreement	90.1	82.4	48.3	66.3	76.5	90.1	74.2	125.8	30.0	27.5
Bartered materials for supplemental stockpile	217.3	83.9	314.7	192.4	200.5	193.3	99.7	37.7	80.0	75.0
Total, Foreign Assistance Programs	1,770.2	1,360.9	1,482.9	1,586.2	1,930.3	2,009.0	1,952.7	1,867.4	1,771.5	1,763.7
Permanent appropriations										
General fund appropriations:										
Removal of surplus agricultural commodities (30% of customs receipts)	168.9	122.9	138.0	89.1	202.6	213.8	130.6	268.7	241.8	311.7
Payments to school funds, Arizona and New Mexico	0.1	0.1	0.1	0.1	0.1	0.1	0.1	0.1	0.1	0.1
Appropriations from special sources:										
Perishable Agricultural Commodities Act fund	0.5	0.6	0.7	0.7	0.8	0.7	0.8	0.8	0.9	0.9

[c] Represents dollar expenditures without deducting value of foreign currencies acquired.

TABLE 1.3 (*continued*)

	1957	1958	1959	1960	1961	1962	1963	1964	Estimated 1965	Estimated 1966
Roads and trails for states, national forests fund	9.7	15.4	8.9	11.9	14.2	10.0	10.9	12.0	13.1	13.4
Expenses, brush disposal	3.4	4.3	4.9	5.0	6.7	6.1	7.6	8.3	9.0	9.5
Restoration of forest lands and improvements	—	—	—	—	—	—	—	—	0.1	0.1
Payments to counties, national grasslands	0.5	0.6	0.5	0.5	0.4	0.4	0.4	0.5	0.5	0.5
Payments to states and territories from the national forests fund	28.5	27.0	22.3	29.8	35.5	25.2	27.4	30.1	33.0	33.7
Establishment of an entomology research laboratory	—	—	—	—	—	—	0.4	—	—	—
Total, Permanent Appropriations	211.6	170.9	175.4	137.1	260.3	256.3	178.1	320.5	298.6	369.9
GRAND TOTAL	5,005.9	4,874.9	7,091.4	5,418.9	5,929.4	6,668.7	7,735.3	7,896.9	7,025.9	6,570.9

SOURCE: *Congress and the Nation*, pp. 670-671.

FIGURE 1.1

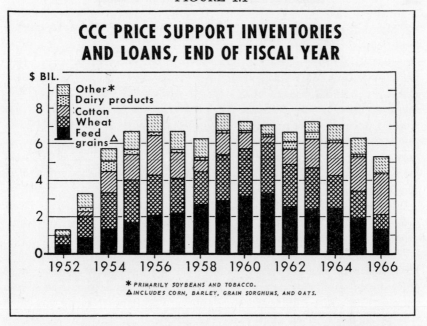

CCC PRICE SUPPORT INVENTORIES AND LOANS, END OF FISCAL YEAR

*PRIMARILY SOYBEANS AND TOBACCO.
△INCLUDES CORN, BARLEY, GRAIN SORGHUMS, AND OATS.

CCC price support inventories and loans, end of fiscal year, 1952-64

Year	Feed grains[1]	Wheat and products	Cotton	Dairy products	Other commodities[2]	Total
	Mil. dol.	Mil. dol.	Mil. dol.	Mil. dol.	Mil. dol.	Mil. dol.
1952	524	364	49	5	379	1,321
1953	816	1,186	321	269	704	3,296
1954	1,339	2,011	1,174	523	720	5,767
1955	1,691	2,329	1,396	330	924	6,670
1956	2,020	2,295	2,162	165	1,027	7,669
1957	2,201	1,915	1,448	161	979	6,704
1958	2,633	1,932	545	142	1,024	6,276
1959	2,880	2,574	1,209	70	974	7,707
1960	3,121	2,615	889	106	593	7,324
1961	3,360	2,707	352	147	473	7,039
1962	2,594	2,292	840	379	552	6,657
1963	2,450	2,329	1,470	418	589	7,256
1964	2,489	1,798	1,751	174	886	7,098

[1] Includes corn, barley, grain sorghums, and oats.
[2] Includes all other commodities under price support, primarily soybeans and tobacco.

Agricultural Stabilization and Conservation Service, *Report of Financial Condition and Operations.*

SOURCE: USDA, *Statistical Handbook*, p. 30.

23

Thus, government efforts toward regulation of agriculture have been less than successful in eliminating surplus stores of agricultural commodities. Price support programs, production controls, surplus disposal programs, and government assistance designed to increase the efficiency of individual farming enterprises have combined to stabilize surpluses to what is, perhaps, the maximum extent permitted by the American value system. This situation is the outgrowth of a national political setting which, at times, has permitted the attainment of certain concessions for agriculture. Furthermore, the value sets of nonfarming Americans have been such as to create sympathy rather than opposition toward the position of the farmer. In short, American values and the American political system have created agricultural policies which have been less than efficient in the strict economic sense of the term. Chronic surpluses have been the result.

Chapter 2 describes how, through the transformation of Public Law 480 into Food for Peace, the United States was able to make agricultural surpluses, which at one time were an economic liability, an asset for United States foreign policy. The remainder of this book will be devoted to an analysis of the 1964 Congressional response to Food for Peace.

United States Foreign Policy and Food for Peace

THE CLOSE OF CHAPTER 1 showed government holdings of surplus agricultural commodities to 1964 remaining at a constant level with a value of about $7 billion. Within the context of American agriculture, and depending on one's point of view, these surpluses may be attributed to the success of agricultural policy in holding the line, or to the failure of this policy to reduce the magnitude of such stocks. As another dimension in the picture of agricultural surpluses, we must now examine how the nation's changing foreign aid policies, together with its surpluses, produced both Public Law 480 and the Food for Peace programs. To study this effectively, one must begin with broad-level discussion of United States aid policy in the postwar world.[1]

UNITED STATES FOREIGN AID POLICY: 1946-1963

From 1945 to 1963, there have been four periods of foreign aid—each one with a different emphasis. The first—1946-1948—may be referred to as the period of *Postwar Relief*. Most of our foreign assistance in these years was provided under a variety of short-term programs aimed at rehabilitation and relief of devastated European areas. The assumption was that the long-range needs of the war-torn countries could be met by such institutions as the International Bank for Reconstruction and the International Monetary Fund. During this period, United States assistance totaled some $14 billion, roughly distributed as follows: capital assistance loan to England in 1947—$3.75 billion; contributions to the United Nations Relief and Rehabilitation Administration amounted to some $2.8 billion; appropriations to the Department of Defense for government and relief in occupied areas resulted in the expenditure of an additional 2.5 billion; the Import-Export Bank made loans of nearly $2 billion, primarily in Europe; and some $1 billion worth of surplus property was sold on credit to the European areas. Assistance to what are now referred to as the underdeveloped nations amounted to very little during this period. Some $2 billion went to the Far East, with Japan receiving half of this assistance; assistance to Latin America consisted only of the continuation of a small technical assistance program begun during the war, a few sales of surplus property, and some $200 million worth of Import-Export Bank loans. Regional aid activities of the United States amounted to some one billion, of which the largest segment was donated in the form of capital to the International Bank for Reconstruction and Development.

Even before 1949, it became evident that the largely *ad hoc* measures described above were not going to be sufficient to combat postwar economic depression, coupled with communist threat in Western Europe. As early as 1947, General George C. Marshall outlined a program (the Marshall Plan) which was to become the heart of the second phase of United States foreign assistance called the *European Recovery Period* (1949-1951). Total United States economic assistance during these years reached some $17.5 billion; Western Europe (including Greece and Turkey) received $13 billion (75 percent) of the total. The remainder of United States assistance during this period was allocated in the following manner: $3 billion to the Far East, of which Japan received one-third; the Philippines about one-half billion dollars and Korea and Taiwan each received approximately $1 billion; assistance to the Near East and Southern Asia amounted to some $350 million, of which India received one-half; assistance to Latin America totaled $600 million.

Attention to defense

During the third period of foreign aid, referred to as the period of *Military Support* (1952-1956), defense considerations were paramount. During these years, military assistance amounted to over 50 percent of all United States aid in contrast to the first five years of the postwar period when a total of less than $1 billion was provided as military assistance to Turkey, Greece and China. Military assistance reached a high of $4 billion—(two-thirds of all assistance)—in 1953 and has declined since that time. Economic assistance during the five-year period averaged some $2.5 billion a year, much of it labeled as defense support. As such, it was directed toward the less-developed countries of the Free World where there were large defensive forces. Assistance to Western Europe (with the exception of Spain and Yugoslavia) declined at this time. Instead, new emphasis was placed upon the Far East where threats of war were growing. Economic aid to the Near East and Southern Asia, especially India and Pakistan, amounted to some 13 percent of total United States bilateral assistance, while assistance to Latin America amounted to 10 percent of the total.

The fourth period is known as the period of *Economic Assistance*. During the years 1956 to 1963, annual economic assistance provided by the United States more than doubled, while the relative importance of military assistance declined. Economic assistance (at $28 billion in 1957 only half as large as military assistance) amounted to three times the military assistance provided in 1963. By 1963, some eighty-seven independent political units, thirty-three of them in Africa, were receiving some form of bilateral economic assistance from the United States. The Near East and Southern Asia received one-third of the total. Economic assistance to Latin America increased to 20 percent of the total; and aid to Africa increased from one percent of the total in 1957, to 10 percent in 1963.

A study of these four periods of foreign aid reveals a distinct shift in United States foreign economic policy from 1946 to 1963. With the close of the war, the Allies assumed that their victory had assured the peace of the world for the indefinite future; therefore, the immediate objective of the United States was to alleviate the economic effects of the war on the participants. This ideal was intensified in the European Recovery Period with the Marshall Plan and the effort to stem the advance of communism in Eastern Europe with extended economic assistance. Realization that the ideal of peace in our time was little more than a myth came early in the 1950's and, during the period of Military Assistance, the United States made a serious effort to contain communism by strengthening defenses of the Free World. After 1956, however, the emphasis of United States foreign aid shifted somewhat to the developing nations of Latin America, Africa, and Asia and away from military assistance to Europe. This change in policy was due primarily to a standoff between the USSR and the United States with respect to the armaments and technological development, and an increasing role of importance, consequently, for the underdeveloped neutralist countries. Competition between the two major powers in the developing areas has been the rationale for our acceptance of a new set of foreign aid objectives which may be summarized in the following manner:[2] First, to assist in the achievement of an international political and economic environment in which the United States can best pursue its own social goals and objectives. Such an objective assumes United States assistance to enable underdeveloped nations of the world to become self-sustaining with respect to political and economic growth; second, to contribute to the internal political stability of governments friendly to the United States by means of economic assistance; third, to contribute to the security from external aggression of the United States and its allies by means of selective economic assistance with the assumption that such aid can influence the international posture of the recipient.

WORLD POPULATION AND FOOD SUPPLY

Since food aid[3] is the focal point of this study, it will be useful to examine, briefly, the worldwide need for food and the way in which United States food assistance coped with this problem. During the last quarter century, man has drastically altered the birth-death ratio in the world. The result has been a sudden population explosion.[4] The world population in 1959-61 exceeded three billion people, and projections based on an anticipated annual compound-growth rate of 1.8 percent point to a world total of 3.6 billion by 1970. The gross size of world population, however, is less of a problem than its distribution.[5] The USDA has estimated that ten subregions of the world will have inadequate supplies of food by 1970, while twelve will have adequate diet. These countries include the following:[6]

Diet-adequate	Diet-deficient
United States	Central America and
Canada	Caribbean
Mexico	Other South America
Brazil[a]	North Africa
River Plate	West Central Africa[b]
Northern Europe	East Africa[b]
Southern Europe	West Asia
Eastern Europe	India
USSR	Other South Asia
Southern Africa	Other East Asia
Japan	Communist Asia
Oceania	

   [a] Brazil has an adequate national-average diet but has many characteristics of diet-deficient subregions. The southern part of the country is much like the River Plate [Río de la Plata] countries; the northeast area probably has an inadequate diet.
   [b] Quality deficiency only.
   Countries in the diet-deficient subregions which show neither quantitative nor qualitative deficiencies in 1959-61 or 1970 include Costa Rica, Trinidad and Tobago, Chile, Cyprus, and Israel.

Twelve subregions are projected to have average diets above the minimum reference standards by 1970. Ten subregions will have diets nutritionally deficient. Two of these will meet the energy [calorie] level but not the other requirements. The other eight will have diets inadequate in quantity and quality.

TABLE 2.1

Population in diet-deficient nations as related to world totals, 1959-61 & projected 1970

	Population				Share of world agricul- tural land pct.	Man- land ratio 1959-61 #/1000 acres
	1959-61 1,000	World share 1959-61 pct.	Annual growth rate 1959-61 to 1970 pct.	1970 1,000		
Central America & Caribbean	32,328	1.1	2.7	42,041	0.6	61
Other South American	51,549	1.7	2.8	67,798	2.1	25
North Africa	84,813	2.8	2.2	105,421	4.7	19
West Central Africa	108,808	3.6	2.1	134,346	6.6	17
East Africa	48,563	1.6	2.3	61,056	5.0	10
West Africa	79,391	2.7	2.4	101,012	5.1	16
India	431,100	14.3	2.2	536,646	4.4	100
Other South Asia	126,397	4.2	2.5	165,755	1.2	108
Communist Asia	712,907	23.7	1.7	846,768	7.4	100
Other East Asia	246,238	8.2	2.5	315,044	1.6	154
Totals	1,922,694	63.9	2.3 (average)	2,375,887	38.7	61 (average)
World totals	3,011,489	100.0	1.8	3,616,259	100.0	31
Food deficit countries as related to world totals	63.8%	63.8%	.5 (difference)	65.7%	38.7	20 (difference)

SOURCE: Based on table 6, p. 14 of USDA, Economic Research Service, Foreign Regional Analysis Division, *The World Food Budget, 1970*, Foreign Agricultural Economic Report #19, October, 1964.

As Table 2.1 illustrates, the bulk of world population is to be found in the diet-deficient regions in spite of an extremely low proportion of agricultural land in these regions. This situation is further complicated by a disproportionate increase in population as compared to food production. As indicated in Table 2.2, food production on the national

FIGURE 2.1

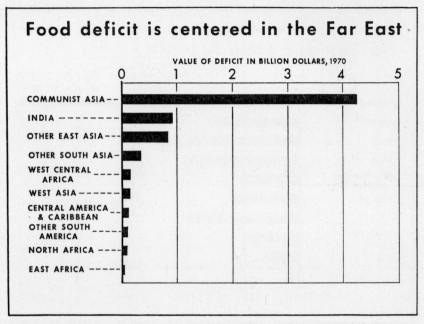

SOURCE: U.S. Department of Agriculture Neg. ERS 3130-64(9) Economic Research Service.

levels in the diet-deficient areas has increased since the late 1930's at a rate of about 20 percent in excess of the rate of increase in the diet-adequate regions. However, when this agricultural productivity is combined with population in terms of per capita food production, as shown in Table 2.3, the rate of increase in the diet-deficient areas drops to only 40 percent of that in the diet-adequate areas. It is, therefore, obvious that increases in food productivity are not going to match population growth rates in the immediate or the foreseeable future. The extent of the resulting food gap, when present estimates are extended to 1970, is illustrated in Figures 2.1 and 2.2.

In terms of international trade, the diet-deficient, underdeveloped countries have been and will be in the foreseeable future, net im-

porters of food. The magnitude of past food imports and 1970 projections is illustrated in Table 2.4.

The following quotation on the balance-of-payments situation,
with respect to the developing nations, clearly establishes the magnitude of world need for food aid.[7]

FIGURE 2.2

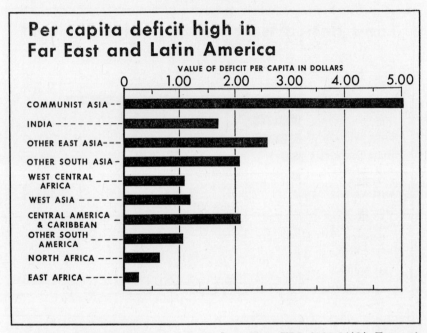

SOURCE: U.S. Department of Agriculture Neg. ERS 3131-64(9) Economic
Research Service.

It is doubtful whether the developing countries will be able to
pay for all these food imports in 1970. The reason is the balance
of payments difficulties which they are experiencing. A sizable gap
in payments of the developing countries had already appeared
before the beginning of the present decade. For the three years,
1958-60, their average annual commodity imports amounted to
U. S. $21,000 million, while their commodity exports amounted to
only $20,000 million. There was, thus, a trade gap of $1,000 million.
In addition, the developing countries had to bear the burden of
other payments, such as investment income and other services, the
net amount of which averaged $4,000 million annually. The total
gap in the current balance of payments of the developing countries
thus amounted to an average of $5,000 million annually during

TABLE 2.2

Trends in food production by subregion, 1935-39, 1952-54, 1959-61 average; 1962, 1963 annual; and projected 1970 (1952-54 = 100)

Subregion	Total production					Average annual change[1]		
	1935-39	1959-61	1962	1963	1970	1935-39 to 1959-61	1952-54 to 1959-61	1959-61 to 1970
						Percent	*Percent*	*Percent*
Diet-adequate								
United States	67	117	119	124	142	3.19	2.41	2.12
Canada	70	104	121	132	134	2.12	0.60	2.83
Mexico	52	157	168	186	236	8.68	8.17	4.99
Brazil	58	141	151	146	195	6.15	5.87	3.85
River Plate	91	99	96	110	126	0.39	-0.18	2.78
Northern Europe	79	116	124	125	137	1.98	2.25	1.83
Southern Europe	85	119	123	123	155	1.75	2.71	3.00
Eastern Europe	119	128	125	124	151	0.32	4.03	1.82
USSR	102	135	141	135	191	1.40	4.94	4.22
Japan	83	146	162	158	206	3.28	6.56	4.15
Oceania	98	118	131	132	152	0.92	2.59	2.91
Southern Africa	n.a.	128	143	n.a.	188	..	4.01	4.70
Total	82	122	127	127	155	2.10	3.11	2.75

[1] Calculated from food production aggregates.

n.a. = not available.

TABLE 2.2 *(continued)*

Subregion	Total production					Average annual change[1]		
	1935-39	1959-61	1962	1963	1970	1935-39 to 1959-61	1952-54 to 1959-61	1959-61 to 1970
						Percent	*Percent*	*Percent*
Diet-deficit								
Central America and Caribbean	58	120	100	96	139	4.66	2.86	1.58
Other South America	60	123	130	131	173	4.50	3.28	4.10
North Africa	68	110	119	122	142	2.70	1.48	2.84
West Central Africa	n.a.	119	123	125	152	..	2.66	2.78
East Africa	n.a.	144	153	158	203	..	6.23	4.12
West Asia	70	116	124	128	143	2.84	2.33	2.33
India	80	126	128	128	167	2.47	3.73	3.23
Other South Asia	82	122	124	129	156	2.15	3.16	2.79
Other East Asia	93	128	140	140	172	1.63	4.00	3.42
Total Free World	78	123	127	129	160	2.50	3.27	3.04
Communist Asia	79	104	109	109	155	1.38	0.59	4.92
Total	78	117	121	123	159	2.10	2.41	3.58
World	81	120	125	125	156	2.10	2.85	3.04

SOURCE: *World Food Budget, 1970*, p. 40.

TABLE 2.3

Trends in food production per capita by subregion (1952-54 = 100)

Subregion	Per capita production						Average annual change[1]		
	1935-39	1959-61	1962	1963	1970		1935-39 to 1959-61	1952-54 to 1959-61	1959-61 to 1970
							Percent	*Percent*	*Percent*
Diet-adequate									
United States	83	104	102	104	110		1.05	0.54	0.62
Canada	91	86	96	103	86		-0.25	-2.00	0.02
Mexico	79	127	128	138	140		2.60	3.88	1.03
Brazil	76	114	114	107	116		2.10	1.98	0.20
River Plate	125	88	82	92	94		-1.29	-1.77	0.76
Northern Europe	92	114	119	119	125		0.99	1.91	1.05
Southern Europe	99	117	118	118	141		0.81	2.37	2.08
Eastern Europe	118	121	116	114	131		0.09	2.95	0.87
USSR	104	123	123	116	152		0.74	3.16	2.45
Japan	102	135	149	144	175		1.37	5.08	2.91
Oceania	127	102	109	107	107		-0.82	0.32	0.51
Southern Africa	n.a.	108	116	n.a.	127		. .	1.17	1.78
Total	94	112	113	111	124		0.80	1.70	1.11

[1] Calculated from food production aggregates.

n.a. = not available.

TABLE 2.3 (continued)

Subregion	Per capita production					Average annual change[1]		
	1935-39	1959-61	1962	1963	1970	1935-39 to 1959-61	1952-54 to 1959-61	1959-61 to 1970
						Percent	Percent	Percent
Diet-deficit								
Central America and Caribbean	78	101	80	75	90	1.29	0.15	-1.10
Other South America	83	102	102	100	109	0.88	0.22	0.72
North Africa	92	94	97	98	97	0.09	-0.86	0.33
West Central Africa	n.a.	103	102	102	106	..	0.40	0.33
East Africa	n.a.	120	120	122	134	..	2.74	1.24
West Asia	86	99	101	102	96	0.61	-0.10	-0.31
India	99	110	106	104	117	0.45	1.38	0.66
Other South Asia	99	103	100	102	103	0.24	0.48	-0.05
Other East Asia	124	108	112	109	113	-0.60	1.07	0.49
Total Free World	97	105	104	103	109	0.32	0.74	0.32
Communist Asia	96	88	90	89	111	-0.37	-1.63	2.54
Total	97	100	99	98	110	0.12	-0.04	1.03
World	97	105	105	104	114	0.28	0.73	0.85

SOURCE: *World Food Budget, 1970*, p. 41.

TABLE 2.4

Commodity composition of food imports into the developing countries from the rest of the world
(1959-61 average and 1970 estimate)

SITC code	Commodity	Value							
		1959-61 average				1970 estimate			
		Latin America	Far East	Near East, Africa*	All developing countries	Latin America	Far East	Near East, Africa*	All developing countries
		Million U.S. dollars							
00	Live animals	15.9	39.8	27.3	83.0	18.8	46.0	68.6	133.4
011	Fresh meat	10.1	17.2	49.7	77.0	22.6	45.4	114.6	182.6
012	Dried meat	10.4	2.2	11.9	24.5	6.4	4.4	24.8	35.6
013	Canned meat	18.9	12.5	42.2	73.6	36.5	17.7	80.6	134.8
022.1	Milk and cream (evaporated or condensed)	10.7	82.8	39.1	132.6	7.8	111.0	87.0	205.8
022.2	Dry milk	12.5	25.2	12.5	50.2	31.4	54.0	26.9	112.3
022.3	Milk and cream (fresh)**	33.3	23.0	39.2	95.5	26.8	36.8	73.1	136.7
023	Butter	6.2	8.8	20.3	35.5	15.8	-9.1	3.6	10.3
024	Cheese and curd	9.3	2.0	26.6	37.9	18.4	-0.4	28.6	46.6
025	Eggs	17.1	13.6	6.7	37.4	10.2	-2.1	19.4	27.5
031	Fish (fresh), etc.**	21.0	6.5	46.7	74.2	16.9	10.4	86.7	114.0
032	Fish (preserved and preparations)**	3.7	17.4	24.4	45.5	3.0	27.9	45.7	76.6
041	Wheat and meslin (unmilled)	149.5	351.8	205.7	707.0	380.0	1,019.8	629.7	2,029.5
042	Rice	26.6	112.7	36.1	175.4	-19.3	297.7	104.2	382.6
043	Barley (unmilled)	4.7	3.8	20.0	28.5	15.1	-16.8	75.1	73.4
044	Maize (unmilled)	7.8	6.2	19.4	33.4	-12.5	21.4	65.6	74.5

TABLE 2.4 (continued)

SITC code	Commodity	Value							
		1959-61 average				1970 estimate			
		Latin America	Far East	Near East, Africa*	All developing countries	Latin America	Far East	Near East, Africa*	All developing countries
045	Other cereals (unmilled)	2.8	3.1	13.6	19.5	5.7	-4.5	44.8	46.0
046	Wheat flour, etc.**	39.1	85.6	160.5	285.2	31.6	137.2	303.8	472.6
047	Flour, etc.*	4.3	8.9	4.6	17.8	3.5	14.3	8.7	26.5
048	Cereal preparations**	32.5	28.9	42.5	103.9	26.2	46.2	79.5	151.9
051-053	Fruits, nuts and products**	20.8	20.1	32.1	73.0	16.8	32.2	60.1	109.1
054-055	Vegetables and products**	42.0	18.6	69.5	130.1	33.9	29.9	130.0	193.8
06	Sugar preparations and honey**	10.9	34.2	168.7	213.8	8.8	54.7	316.2	379.7
07	Coffee, tea, cocoa and spices**	2.6	13.7	38.0	54.3	2.1	22.0	71.1	95.2
08	Feedstuffs**	13.0	7.7	15.9	36.6	10.5	12.3	29.6	52.4
09	Miscellaneous food preparations**	35.1	25.3	46.1	106.5	28.3	40.4	86.9	155.6
11	Beverages**	21.4	24.5	115.4	161.3	17.3	39.3	214.7	271.3
121	Tobacco (unmanufactured)	12.0	27.2	30.2	69.4	23.2	7.1	48.7	79.0
122	Tobacco (manufactured)**	21.8	36.7	59.1	117.6	17.6	58.8	111.3	187.7
0 and 1	Total food imports	616.0	1,060.0	1,424.0	3,100.0	803.4	2,154.0	3,039.6	5,997.0

* Not elsewhere specified.
** Marked items are based on United Nations Commodity trade statistics; unmarked items are based on FAO Commodity review 1964.

SOURCE: The Demand for Food, and Conditions Governing Food Aid During Development, pp. 16-17.

1958-60. This was met by an inflow of long-term capital, both public and private, and official donations, including food aid from the developed countries.

The gap in the balance of payments of the developing countries is expected to widen as development proceeds in these countries. This is partly because of the increasing import requirements arising out of the development plans of these countries and partly because of their inability to expand their export earnings sufficiently. *The World Economic Survey* estimated that the import requirements of the developing countries from the rest of the world may amount to $41,000 million. . . .

On the other hand, the export earnings of the countries from the rest of the world in 1970 are estimated to be only U. S. $29,000, or, at best, $31,000 million. Thus, the developing countries in 1970 may face a trade gap of at least $10,000 million. To this must be added the payments for investment income and for other services which the developing countries will have to bear, and the net burden of which is estimated at $8,000 million, or, on a reduced estimate, $7,000 million. Thus, the total gap in the balance of payments of the developing countries in 1970 may amount to as much as $17,000 million. This is the best estimate at present available. However, it is often considered to err on the higher side, mainly because of not taking into account the likelihood of the developing countries developing several import substitutes. This may be so, or this may be merely wishful thinking. In any case, even if it leads to a reduction of the gap, say by $3,000 million or $4,000 million, the balance of payments gap of the developing countries in 1970 will still be almost twice as large as their total import needs of food, which are estimated at $6,550 million. It is for this reason that it is doubtful whether the developing countries will be able to pay for all of their food import requirements in 1970, unless, of course, they severely cut down some other import needs. . . .

Thus, in the absence of food aid, the developing countries will either be forced to cut back import of nonfood items necessary for continued economic development, or restrict food requirements which are already at a dangerously low level.

The explanation of why the developing nations, suffering from a food deficit, have thus far been able to avoid disastrous starvation lies in the massive food aid they have received from nations with food surpluses.[8] Most of this aid originated in the United States. From July 1, 1954 to June 30, 1964, the United States contributed some $14 billion worth of food aid under four programs as depicted in Table 2.5. During this same period, food aid from the other donor countries of the world amounted to some $300 million. About two-thirds of this latter total has been contributed by Canada in the form of wheat and wheat flour. Australia and France have contributed lesser but significant quantities. Since the endorsement of the United Nations World Food Program in 1960, some sixty nations have made commitments to donate food to the program.

TABLE 2.5

United States commitments of surplus agricultural commodities 1 July 1954-30 June 1964

Type of program	Market value (in millions of dollars)
1. Sales for local currency under:	
(a) PL 480	9,950
(b) Mutual Security Act	2,000
2. Grants for disaster and other relief	1,675
3. Grants for economic development	125
4. Sales under long-term credits	250
Total	14,000

SOURCE: United States House of Representatives; Extension and Amendment of Public Law 480. Report No. 1767, 88th Congress, 2nd Session and Monthly Operations Reports, International Co-operation Administration.

PUBLIC LAW 480

The postwar trends of United States agricultural and foreign policy, stimulated by world food problems, resulted in a demand which received strong support in the United States Congress in 1953-54.[9] One of the results of Congressional concern over this problem was the Agricultural Trade Development and Assistance Act of 1954, or Public Law 480.

McLellan and Clare[10] have traced the idea of matching United States agricultural surpluses with the food needs of the world to the 1952 National Conference of the American Farm Bureau Federation in Seattle, Washington. The rationale of the proposal was that countries having dollar surpluses, but preferring to use them for capital purchases, would be willing to buy United States surplus agricultural products for local currencies. As a result, it was asserted, the effective demand for United States agricultural products would be expanded and United States surpluses reduced. It would appear, therefore, that United States domestic interests were paramount in the initial idea of

Public Law 480. During a 1953 conference, the Farm Bureau actually did support legislative action for sales of agricultural surpluses for foreign currencies. Then early in July 1953, another event of considerable import to the origin of Public Law 480 took place:

> On July 16, 1953, hearings were called by the Senate Committee on Agriculture and Forestry to consider S. 2249, a bill to give the President emergency authority to use surplus agricultural commodities for famine assistance in various countries in need. The early part of these hearings was devoted to discussion of specific provisions of the bill; however, with the testimony of Senator Hubert Humphrey, the hearings took a new tack. He made a strong plea for a greatly expanded program of surplus utilization. . . .
> Senator Humphrey outlined a multifaceted program which included donations, sales at world market prices, sales at concessional prices, long-term loans, sales for native currencies and trade of commodities for strategic stockpile materials. He also recommended the utilization of voluntary relief organizations wherever possible. . . .
> . . . Many bills had been introduced into both Houses of Congress in the past which described various methods of surplus utilization. Most of these former proposals, however, were concerned with only one or two channels of distribution with far less complex and limited goals. Senator Humphrey recognized these proposals in his remarks and suggested that they be studied with the objective of incorporating them into a major program for increased utilization of farm products throughout the world.[11]

On July 22, 1953, the Senate Committee on Agriculture and Forestry met in Executive session and appointed a subcommittee to draft a bill for the disposal of surplus agricultural commodities. The bill (S. 2475) was introduced in the Senate by Senator Andrew F. Schoeppel (R-Kansas) on July 24, 1953 and reported out the same day with a "do pass without amendment" recommendation.

The Senate action met with initial opposition on the part of the Eisenhower Administration. For example, in a 1953 letter to Senator Aiken, Secretary of Agriculture Ezra Taft Benson commented that the farm products section of the foreign aid legislation provided sufficient "opportunity, on a trial basis, to see whether we can effectively sell our agricultural surpluses for foreign currencies. . . . If we find this feasible, we will give broader support to programs of this kind."[12]

In spite of this opposition, the Senate passed the bill by a voice vote and referred it to the House Committee on Agriculture on July

29. The House, however, failed to act prior to adjournment, and the bill was carried over to the second session in 1954. In the meantime, during the April 1954 House hearings on farm legislation, the Administration reversed its stand by asking for authorization to use one billion dollars worth of surplus commodities for foreign aid during a three-year period.

A matter for debate

On June 9, 1954, a substitute version of S. 2475 was reported out of the House Committee on Agriculture. The House Committee amendments, however, dealt mostly with details and did little to modify the substance of the Senate proposal. When the bill was debated on the floor of the House, many congressmen expressed their concern.[13] Karl C. King (R-Pennsylvania) said the measure put "the finishing touches on the purest socialistic scheme ever perpetrated on this country." Jacob K. Javits (R-New York) opposed the proposal because it had the effect of "masking the loss" of the Commodity Credit Corporation in overseas operations. Augustine B. Kelly (D-Pennsylvania) and Martin Dies (D-Texas) felt that the definition of friendly nations was not stringent enough. Page Belcher (R-Oklahoma) opposed the measure because he thought it was a "giveaway program." Thomas G. Abernathy (D-Mississippi), Jamie L. Whitten (D-Mississippi), Fred Marshall (D-Minnesota), and W. R. Poage (D-Texas) all supported the bill but expressed the fear that the program would reduce United States commercial incentives in agriculture.

Twenty amendments to the committee bill were accepted on the floor of the House. However, when the conference committee met on June 30 to iron out the differences between the two Houses, most of the House amendments were deleted. Both Houses subsequently accepted the decisions of this committee. When President Eisenhower signed S. 2475 into Public Law 480 on July 10, 1954, he commented that the legislation would "lay the basis for a permanent expansion of our exports of agricultural products, with lasting benefits to ourselves and peoples in other lands."[14]

As first enacted, Public Law 480 had three titles. Title I authorized the sale of surplus agricultural commodities to foreign countries for payment in the currencies of these countries. Use of the currencies thus received was strictly limited by the provisions of the law. Title II provided for the donations of supplies of emergency food to victims in disaster areas. Food assistance has also been used under this title to supplement children's diets and to provide food wages for economic development programs. Title III was divided into two programs. Under the first, provision was made for the donation of food to welfare organizations which administer and distribute the food through independent programs. The second program under Title III allowed the CCC to barter supplies of surplus agricultural commodities for goods required by the national stockpiles of the United States. In 1959, a new title (IV) was added to Public Law 480 providing for sales of surplus foods for long-term low interest notes with repayment being made to the United States in dollars after periods of up to twenty years.

From 1954 to 1960, Public Law 480 was modified several times by legislation.[15] In general, the effect of most of this legislation was to expand the program beyond the original limits of the law.

FOOD FOR PEACE

By 1960, a small group in the Senate, headed by Senator Hubert H. Humphrey, had begun to make progress in their effort to transform Public Law 480 so as to correspond more closely with the aforementioned shift in United States foreign assistance policy,[16] i.e., the movement toward economic aid to developing nations. This struggle is at the heart of the Food for Peace program, for it was the effort of Senator Humphrey to transform the largely surplus disposal Public Law 480 program into a major instrument of foreign policy. Humphrey's first proposal to use American agricultural surpluses "to promote the attainment of an honorable peace" was presented to the Senate Committee on Agriculture and Forestry in the form of S. 3020, which was introduced at the early date of February 25, 1954. The bill died in committee. Early in 1956, Senator Humphrey was authorized to conduct an intensive study of the Public Law 480 program. He submitted his findings to the committee on February 18, 1958, in a report entitled "Food and Fiber as a Force for Freedom." This report was critical of the surplus disposal aspects of the Public Law 480 program. It urged multiyear programming so as to make Public Law 480 assistance more useful for recipient nations and recommended establishment of a coordinating officer—a "Food for Peace Administrator" with the status of special assistant to the President in the White House office. Humphrey's report was not well received; it ran into opposition from the committee *per se,* from the Farm Bureau, and from the Republican Administration. Humphrey, however, persisted, and on April

16, 1959, he introduced S. 1711, a bill which embodied the recommendations of his report. On April 20, an identical bill was introduced into the House by Lester R. Johnson (D-Wisconsin). By now, perhaps skeptical of the sympathy of the Senate Agriculture Committee toward food aid, Humphrey submitted his bill as a foreign relations bill and, thus, secured the referral of it to the Senate Committee on Foreign Relations.

In July committee hearings on S. 1711, both the Department of State and the Department of Agriculture criticized the proposal on the ground that it would contribute to the continuation of our agricultural surpluses. Thus, on August 7, 1959, the bill was reported out of committee with several modifications: the provision for a five-year program was reduced to three; the provision for long-term (ten-year) programming commitments was dropped; and the committee recommended that coordination of the program come from the Department of Agriculture rather than from the White House office.

The President's program

In his special farm message to Congress on January 29, 1959, President Eisenhower initiated a "Food for Peace Program," apparently to counteract Senator Humphrey's efforts to modify Public Law 480. Subsequently, Don Paarlberg was appointed as White House coordinator of the program, but his duties fell short of those recommended by Senator Humphrey. Following this appointment, the Republican Administration was in a position to oppose Humphrey's proposals as superfluous.

During the same period, proposals were being considered for the regular extension of Public Law 480. Senator Ellender used his prerogative as chairman of the Agriculture Committee to see that S. 1748 was debated on the floor prior to the Humphrey proposal, which effectively killed S. 1711 since both proposals dealt with the same legislative program. Senator Humphrey's persistence, however, resulted in the incorporation of some of his proposals into the Public Law 480 program, for he submitted S. 1711 section by section to both the Committee on Agriculture and Forestry and on the floor of the Senate as amendments to the bill for the extension of Public Law 480. Thus Senator Humphrey managed to obtain a provision for a three-year extension of Public Law 480 and an agreement to change the short title of Public Law 480 to "Food for Peace Act of 1959." While the former passed on the floor, the latter failed. Most of the debate surrounding the Humphrey amendments centered on the issue of whether the nature of Public Law 480 was foreign or domestic. In conference, substantial disagreement developed on the Public Law 480 bill, since an effort corresponding to that made in the Senate by Humphrey had not been made in the House. The result in the final bill was a two-year extension and incorporation of the long-term supply provisions Humphrey had proposed.

The final step in the evolution of Food for Peace came with the election of John F. Kennedy to the Presidency. Even in campaign speeches, Kennedy had expressed enthusiasm for using Food for Peace —stating, for example, at Mitchell, South Dakota:

> I don't regard the . . . agricultural surplus as a problem, I regard it as an opportunity . . . not only for our own people, but for people all around the world.
>
> Fellow Americans facing a difficult future, . . . I think the farmers can bring more credit, more lasting goodwill, more chance for freedom, more chance for peace, than almost any other group of Americans in the next ten years, if we recognize that food is strength, and food is peace, and food is freedom, and food is a helping hand to people around the world whose goodwill and friendship we want.[17]

This commitment to Food for Peace was more than an idle campaign promise, for Kennedy's second Executive order as President on January 24, 1961, established the White House Office of Food for Peace in accord with the original Humphrey recommendations. George S. McGovern, appointed by President Kennedy as the first director of the Food for Peace program, relates the following:

> A few weeks later, the 1960 campaign ended with John F. Kennedy the winner by a narrow margin. His own victory had scarcely been confirmed when he telephoned me . . . to express regret over my defeat in the race for the U.S. Senate. He suggested that I talk with him after he returned to Washington before making any plans. On December 16, he asked me to serve as director of a newly proposed White House Office of Food for Peace to strengthen the use of our agricultural surpluses as a constructive instrument of American foreign policy.[18]

The emphasis on the new program[19] has continued under the Johnson Administration. Richard W. Reuter, McGovern's successor as director, has ably followed the pattern established by the counsel of Senator Humphrey.

Although many writers and administrators equate Food for Peace with Public Law 480, a connotative difference should be noted between the two terms. Whereas the aims of the original Public Law 480 were primarily domestic, and thus directed toward the alleviation of United States agricultural surpluses, Food for Peace emphasized the role of food aid as an instrument of American foreign policy. It was Senator Humphrey who realized the trend of foreign assistance policy and the magnitude of the food problems of the world. It was he also who conceived of matching American agricultural overabundance with the requirements of foreign policy and a humanitarian solution to human needs all over the world. The specification of a Food for Peace program by the Eisenhower Administration and the revision and implementation of this program by the Kennedy and Johnson Administrations, were an indication that the Executive had reached an accord with Humphrey's ideals—albeit some five years in the process.

FOOD FOR PEACE IMPLEMENTATION[20]

The broad Food for Peace policy goals are implemented by a cooperative effort on the part of various government agencies specified by law and delegation of authority. Most of the administration of Public Law 480 is handled by three major actors: (1) the United States Department of Agriculture (USDA), acting directly through the Secretary of Agriculture and redelegation of authority to the Commodity Credit Corporation; (2) the United States Department of State which has delegated the bulk of its authority and responsibility to the Agency for International Development (AID); and (3) the Director of Food for Peace, who is a Special Assistant to the President and functions in a coordinative capacity.[21]

Practically speaking, interaction among these agencies is informal. There is, however, a decision-making unit within which the interaction is formalized for all programs except Title II emergency assistance. This is the Interagency Staff Committee (ISC), established in 1954 by the Secretary of Agriculture, acting under Presidential directive to insure effective coordination of Public Law 480 operations. The membership of this committee includes representatives of the following: (1) Department of Agriculture, (2) Department of State, (3) Agency for International Development, (4) Bureau of the Budget, (5) Department of the Treasury, (6) Department of Commerce, (7) United States Information Agency, and (8) Office of Emergency Planning. The committee is chaired by a representative of the Secretary of Agriculture and a representative of the Director of the Food for Peace Office attends meetings as an observer.[22]

Under Title I of Public Law 480,[23] the President is authorized to carry out agreements with friendly nations in order to provide for the sale of United States surplus agricultural commodities for foreign currencies. Actual movement of Title I commodities is through private trade channels. Title I rates are financed by the CCC through letters of commitment to United States banks. The attempt is made under Title I agreements not to disrupt cash marketings, world prices, or normal channels of trade. Foreign currencies accruing to the United States under Title I are generally used in two different fashions, referred to as "United States uses" and "country uses." Title I currency reserved for United States use may, upon the discretion of this nation, be used for purposes such as the following: payment of United States obligations abroad; United States expenses in recipient countries; agricultural market development; buildings for United States government use; trade fairs; international education; cultural exchange; distribution of books overseas; translation and collection of scientific works; and support of research activities. Such expenditure of currencies are charged to the appropriations of the Agency for International Development. Under ordinary circumstances, the law specifies that at least 10 percent of foreign currency returns from any specific agreement must be earmarked for United States use. In practice, however, the amount is usually larger, unless the United States holds surpluses of such currencies (which is usually the case). With respect to the "country uses" of foreign currencies, a portion of the returns from Title I agreements is designated in the original sales agreement for foreign aid to the recipient country. Included in this provision are local currency development loans, development grants, assistance for the common defense, and "Cooley loans" which provide that up to 25 percent of the proceeds from each sales agreement may be set aside for loans to private enterprise. With the exception of development grants, these funds are available for use without appropriation and a waiver of appropriation is authorized for development grants also.

Authority is delegated

The President delegated his vested authority for execution of Public Law 480 to several governmental agencies in Executive Order 10900 as amended.[24] By this order, the Secretary of Agriculture is vested with the authority and responsibility for the administration of

Title I, except where alternative delegation has been made. The Secretary of Agriculture is also charged with determining which agricultural commodities are in surplus under Section 106 of Public Law 480. Two broad exceptions to the authority of the Secretary of Agriculture are noted in Executive Order 10900: (1) subject to the direction of the President, the Director of the Food for Peace program "shall be responsible for the continuous supervision and coordination of the functions herein above delegated or otherwise assigned to officers or agencies of the Government,"[25] and (2) "all functions under the Act, however vested, delegated, or assigned are subject to the responsibilities of the Secretary of State with respect to the foreign policy of the United States as such policy relates to such functions."[26]

The main decision-making body with respect to the Title I program is the ISC which reviews all Title I proposals on a regular basis in order to coordinate the various interests of the proposals with the appropriate government agencies. Factors considered by the ISC in developing a Title I agreement include the following:

(1) the participating country's needs, economic status, and foreign exchange position; (2) the impact on dollar sales and other export programs; (3) effect on export markets of other supplying countries; and (4) the relationship of the program to the foreign aid program and overall foreign policies of the United States.[27]

Under Title II provision is made for agricultural surplus commodities held in CCC stocks to be used for famine relief and other purposes. Essentially, two types of program are authorized respectively under Sections 201 and 202 of Public Law 480.[28] Section 201 authorizes use of CCC stocks of surplus commodities to meeting famine or other extraordinary food requirements in foreign nations.[29] Such assistance may be provided either for the people of friendly nations or to friendly but needy peoples without regard to the friendliness of the governments. Section 202 programs authorize the use of CCC stocks of surplus commodities for meeting food requirements of needy peoples and for the promotion of economic development. Such programs are undertaken in conjunction with friendly governments, voluntary relief agencies, or through intergovernmental organizations such as the World Food Program and the United Nations Children's Fund. In the administering of Section 202 programs, the law specifies that care must be taken to avoid interference with sales which otherwise might have been made.

The vast bulk of the administrative responsibility for Title II programs rests within the AID. Executive Order 10900, as amended,[30] delegated responsibility for Title II programs to the Secretary of State, who (by Delegation of Authority No. 104 as amended),[31] redelegated the responsibility to the administrator of AID. This administrator, under the provisions of Delegation of Authority No. 23,[32] passed on the prescribed functions to the regional assistant administrators and to the assistant administrator for material resources. This transfer of authority was supplemented by a memorandum entitled "Administration of the Agricultural Trade Development and Assistance Act of 1954, as amended (Public Law 480)."[33] The Department of Agriculture, however, determines which commodities are surplus and advises AID personnel in recipient countries of their availability for Title II programs. The USDA also arranges for ocean transportation of Title II commodities by AID request.

For quick decisions

The emergency nature of Section 201 assistance requires speedy decision-making on the part of the donor; hence, most such decisions are made by AID personnel in the field, and the regular decision-making channels of Food for Peace are largely bypassed.[34] In Section 202 Title II programs, administration is more complex and time-consuming because the emergency factor is absent. Assistance is offered on a grant basis for wages in food for economic development work, sustenance to families and livestock, stimulation of livestock development programs, and child-feeding and maternal-child health programs. As in the case of Section 201 programs, the role of the AID mission within the recipient country is important. The missions initiate proposals for specific Title II programs, evaluate program proposals submitted to them by cooperating sponsors, assist cooperating sponsors in the development of program proposals, and coordinate the programs with our overall foreign aid objectives. In addition, the mission determines whether the agendas are adequately planned and financed, and obtains approval of the foreign country involved for the initiation of such programs.

Section 202 programs are coordinated with the foreign aid objectives of the United States by the Regional Bureau of AID in Washington. Policy guidelines, however, are formulated by the Office of Material Resources of AID, which also supervises implementation and auditing procedures and presents the AID case before the Interagency Staff Committee which must ultimately approve all such programs.

Title III also authorizes two general types of program; Sections 302 and 303.[35] The former amends and broadens the authority under Section 416 of the Agricultural Act of 1949, for surplus food donations to be distributed in the United States to needy persons and elsewhere, and overseas to the needy through nonprofit voluntary agencies and intergovernmental organizations. Section 303 provides for barter of CCC surplus stocks with foreign countries for strategic and other materials, goods, and equipment.

Domestic distribution and barter of surpluses obviously have little to do with fostering peace through food aid, and need not be discussed here.[36] These procedures merely add to the government arsenal of surplus disposal instruments.

Under the foreign donation program of Section 302, the United States government donates surplus foodstuffs to nongovernmental distributing agencies, i.e., nonprofit voluntary agencies and intergovernmental organizations,[37] which, in turn, distribute food on a "people-to-people" basis.[38] These commodities assist needy persons and school children, are available to distributing agencies and social institutions within the recipient country, and to programs of relief, rehabilitation, and reconstruction in the fields of health, welfare, education, agriculture, industry, emigration, and resettlement.

Division of functions

Statutory governmental responsibility for Title III donation programs is vested in the CCC, but since this is not an administrative body, these functions have been divided between AID and USDA in the following manner:

Responsibility for the program for the donation of commodities under legislation cited in this part is in the Department [of Agriculture]. However, in the conduct of the program the Department will utilize the personnel and facilities of AID in the performance of certain administrative functions. The administrative functions to be performed by the Department and those to be performed by AID will be substantially as outlined below.

(I) *Functions of the Department.* The Department will:

(i) Determine the commodities and quantities thereof available for donation.

(ii) Approve requests for commodities against approved programs and arrange for procurement, processing, reprocessing, packaging, container marking, and delivery of commodities in accordance therewith.

(iii) Have responsibility for claims.

(II) *Functions of AID.* AID will:
(i) Evaluate, coordinate, approve or arrange for approval of distributing agencies' proposed foreign country programs.
(ii) Administer United States Government overseas activities.
(iii) Assist and provide program direction to distributing agencies.
(iv) Review and audit the overseas operations of distributing agencies.[39]

A major portion of the responsibility for Title III programs rests with the distributing agencies. In general terms, the distributing agencies are responsible for program formulation and the handling and proper use of Title III commodities from the time they acquire title until such commodities are consumed by the recipients. In case of misuse, damage, or loss, the agencies are held liable by the USDA. Within each recipient country, must be a qualified representative of the agencies who implements the program. The agencies require a staff competent for administration of the program. This staff, however, may be composed of indigenous nationals.

Final administrative responsibility for Title III programs is with the Interagency Staff Committee which reviews and acts on each proposal. In practice, most of the work is done by a review committee which is a subcommittee of the ISC. This committee, which examines each proposal in detail and makes recommendations to the ISC, is composed of representatives of the Foreign Agricultural Service of the Department of Agriculture, the Bureau of the Budget, the Department of State (Bureau of Economic Affairs), and AID (Office of Material Resources, Food for Peace Division, and the appropriate Regional Bureau). On occasion, other representatives may sit on the committee also.

Title IV,[40] added to Public Law 480 on September 29, 1959, authorizes sales of surplus agricultural commodities for dollars on a long-term credit basis, subject to the stipulation that such commodities are to be utilized for domestic consumption in the recipient country.[41] Under this program, the United States government is authorized to enter into agreements for the delivery of surplus agricultural commodities. These agreements may obligate the contractual partners for as long as ten years. Credit may be extended to the recipient of Title IV commodities for periods of up to twenty years. Two general types of Title IV programs exist: "government-to-government" sales, and "government-to-private-trade" sales.

Delegations of authority and the processing of Title IV proposals are identical to those of Title I, with the exception of participation by the National Advisory Council in Title IV agreements. On a case-by-case basis, the National Advisory Council determines the payment period and the rates of interest, which, however, must not exceed the cost to the United States Treasury.

MAGNITUDE OF FOOD FOR PEACE OPERATIONS

Food for Peace operations are large by any standard. (For a comparison with other aid programs, see Appendix I.) During the ten-year period from July 1, 1954 through December 31, 1964, commitments have been made for shipment of more than $17 billion worth of surplus commodities under all four Titles of Public Law 480. As Table 2.6 depicts, 61.9 percent of this total has been under Title I. Titles II, III, and IV have accounted for 10.4 percent, 25.2 percent and 2.3 percent of the total, respectively. During this same period, commodities with an export market value of $12.3 billion were actually shipped under all four Titles. This amounted to approximately 27 percent of all agricultural exports during the same period. The amounts of wheat and rice exported under Public Law 480 are particularly significant. Public Law 480 shipments of wheat in 1964 constituted 43 percent of the total 1963 United States wheat harvest, while 1964 rice shipments amounted to 30 percent.[42]

What portion of these shipments may be considered as foreign aid, and what portion credited as concessional sales? While all Title I programs are theoretically sales, the practice of granting, loaning, and spending the proceeds in recipient countries makes these foreign aid programs, at least in the short run.

From July 1, 1954 through June 30, 1964 (because of the period of time differential, the following data are not strictly comparable with those in Table 2.6), Title I sales agreements amounted to the equivalent of $9,403.2 million. Of this amount, some $8,289.4 million had actually been collected as of June 30, 1964. Disbursements of such currencies by the United States government amounted, however, to only $5,279.4 million during the same period.[43] Therefore there is a discrepancy of $3,010.0 million between collections and disbursements. This is the amount of Title I currencies which the United States government, for one reason or another, has been unable to spend. Such currencies, therefore, represent a part of the total magnitude of the financial concessions the United States makes to recipient nations under Title I programs. The remaining portion of such financial concessions emerges

TABLE 2.6

Public Law 480 commitments[1] to export U.S. farm commodities, July 1, 1954 through Dec. 31, 1964
(in millions of dollars)[2]

Fiscal year	Title I Sales for local currencies	Title II Disaster relief and other assistance[3]	Title III Foreign donations	Barter	Title IV Long-term dollar sales	Total all titles
1955	354.6	107.8	197.2	124.6	—	784.2
1956	671.3	101.0	302.5	298.4	—	1,373.2
1957	1,034.6	131.2	253.7	400.5	—	1,820.0
1958	727.8	109.5	272.5	99.8	—	1,209.6
1959	831.3	77.8	209.8	132.3	—	1,251.2
1960	1,128.0	85.7	148.9	149.2	—	1,511.8
1961[4]	1,792.3	270.9	208.2	143.9	—	2,415.3
1962	1,590.3	212.1	224.5	198.4	57.1	2,282.4
1963	1,227.0	331.6	277.3	60.1	88.6	1,984.6
1964	617.7	282.3	334.6	112.2	118.3	1,465.1
1965 (1st half)	633.9	87.4	140.1	47.9	131.1	1,040.4
Total	10,608.8[5]	1,797.3	2,569.3	1,767.3	395.1	17,137.8

[1] As used herein, "Commitments" refers to sales agreements under Title I and Title IV, transfer authorizations under Title II, and Title III shipments under barter contracts and foreign donation authorizations. In some instances, Title I and Title IV agreements provide for multiyear programming. Total commitments shown for each fiscal year do not necessarily correspond with actual shipments during the same period.

[2] Export market value (includes certain transportation costs) is used for Title I, Title III barter and Title IV. Title II transfer authorizations and Title III foreign donations are at CCC cost.

[3] Includes child-feeding, economic development and World Food Program.

[4] Includes financing for last 3 years of 4-year India agreement signed May 4, 1960.

[5] Estimated market value calculated on ratio of current market prices to CCC cost, $837.4 million (all figures also include authorized ocean freight costs on Title III foreign donations).

SOURCE: U.S. Congress, House, *Annual Report on Activities Carried on Under Public Law 480, 83rd Congress, 89th Congress, 1st session,* 1965, p. 98.

when currency disbursements are analyzed.[44] Of the $5,279.4 million worth of currencies disbursed under Title I programs as of June 30, 1964, 11.9 percent was used for the common defense of the recipient nations; 16.5 percent was granted back to the recipient countries for use in economic development; 2.6 percent was loaned to private enterprises within the recipient nations; and 48.4 percent was loaned back to the recipient nations under long-term credit arrangements. United States uses of Title I currencies amounted to only 20.3 percent of the total disbursed. Thus of the $8,289.4 million worth of currencies actually collected under Title I program, $3,010 (36.3%) have not been used (which must be considered an economic concession to the recipient), and $4,200.4 million (7.97%) of currencies disbursed have been used for the benefit of recipient nations or returned to them. Hence, some 87.0 percent of all Title I programs may be considered directly as foreign aid. The remaining 13.0 percent which has been devoted to United States uses, it should be remembered, was spent in recipient countries and thus represents a concession to the recipient nations. In theory, much of this latter expenditure will ultimately be recovered by the United States. Furthermore, Title I programs have expanded normal commercial markets for United States agricultural commodities. Nevertheless, as of 1964, it is legitimate to speak of Title I as foreign aid rather than as a business operation.

When the above data are combined with the totals of Table 2.6, it becomes possible to estimate the extent to which Public Law 480 is a foreign aid program. Assuming that Title I falls entirely under the foreign aid category, as do Title II and Title III foreign donation programs, one can conclude that some 87.2 percent of all sales during the first ten years of Public Law 480 operations were basically foreign aid.

Chapter 3

The Congressional Image of Public Law 480

IT IS CHARACTERISTIC of human behavior—individual or collective— that perceptions are functionally selective. Our image of the present is very often determined by the experiences of the past. Accordingly, the perspectives from which Congress and the Executive viewed Public Law 480 and Food for Peace were not only different, or even antithetical at times, but probably were determined by past experiences. Since the chief purpose of this study is to examine the politics of Food for Peace as reflected in Congressional decision making during 1964, a survey of Congressional attitudes toward Public Law 480 from its inception is imperative in order to understand the Congressional perception of the program in 1964.

SURVEY OF CONGRESSIONAL ATTITUDES TOWARD PUBLIC LAW 480

With a few exceptions, Congressional attitudes have centered on the temporary character of Titles I and II which require periodic extensions. The necessity of such extensions has served as the rationale for periodic Congressional reexaminations of Public Law 480. Four such extensions took place prior to 1964: the first in 1957, the second in 1958, the third in 1959, and the fourth in 1961. The 1957 and 1959 extensions were the most crucial in developing the Congressional image of Public Law 480. Under the provisions of the original act, which set the terminal date for Titles I and II at June 30, 1957, the $700 million authorized for Title I was soon considered by Congress to be inadequate and thus in 1955, Congress added an $800 million authorization to the program and in 1956, $1.5 billion more. An additional $2 billion was added in 1961 as supplementary authorization for Title I. During the same period, there was only one supplementary authorization for Title II—$200 million in 1956. This addition, however, cannot be counted as a significant part of the expansion of the

Title II program, since, in the regular extension of the program in 1958, there was no allocation of funds whatsoever for Title II. With these exceptions, no Congressional authorization has occurred for either Title I or II programs, beyond those specified in the extension. Title III programs were made permanent under the 1954 provisions. Table 3.1 depicts the extensions and authorizations for Titles I and II which preceded 1964.

These data might be expected to provide an index of the general Congressional attitude which prevailed toward the program prior to 1964. However, they did not. The three-year provision for Titles I and II, contained in the original law, may be explained in terms of the general enthusiasm which surrounded the enactment of Public Law 480. In adding $800 million to Title I authorizations in August of 1955, Congress complained that the Executive was too cautious in its implementation of the program. Congress, specified, therefore, that the additional authorization was to be considered not only as a limitation but also an objective. Again in 1956, Congress—with the provision of an additional $1.5 billion for Title I and $200 million for Title II—expressed a concern that the complete potential of the program was not being recognized.

Congressional attitude changes

By the time the original three-year program had expired in 1957, however, the general attitude of Congress had changed. The Republican Administration, earlier hesitant to implement the program to the extent of Congressional desires, still was dragging its feet. The first session of the Eighty-Fifth Congress, apparently in agreement that the program was getting out of hand, extended Titles I and II for only one year and continued Title I authorizations at the level then current. The Title II program, however, was expanded. The 1958 extension, however, while expanding Title I, failed to provide additional funds for Title II because previous authorizations had not been used up. Subsequent extensions of the program seemed to reflect a guarded Congressional optimism about Public Law 480. With the beginning of Food for Peace in 1961, Congress returned to its initial enthusiasm for the program. As the data in Table 3.1 indicate, however, the 1961 extension merely continued a trend of cautious expansion of Public Law 480 operations.

On the basis of a simple trend analysis, one would have expected further expansion of Public Law 480 and Food for Peace programs by

TABLE 3.1

Authorizations: Titles I and II, the Agricultural Trade Development and Assistance Act of 1954

Public law and Congress nos.	Effective	Program period	Authorization[1]		Period of extension both titles	Annual authorizations	
			Title I	Title II		Title I	Title II
			Mil. Dol.	Mil. Dol.	years	Mil. Dol.	Mil. Dol.
480, 83d	July 10, 1954	Through June 30, 1957	700	300	3	—	—
387, 84th	Aug. 12, 1955	Through June 30, 1957	800	—	—	—	—
962, 84th	Aug. 3, 1956	Through June 30, 1957	1,500	200[2]	—	1,000	166.6
128, 85th	Aug. 13, 1957	July 1, 1957–June 30, 1958	1,000	300	1	1,000	300
931, 85th	Sept. 6, 1958	July 1, 1958–Dec. 31, 1959	2,250	—	1½	2,250	—[5]
341, 86th	Sept. 21, 1959	Jan. 1, 1960–Dec. 31, 1961	3,000	600	2	—	—
28, 87th	May 4, 1961	Through Dec. 31, 1961	2,000	—	—	2,500	300
128, 87th	Aug. 8, 1961	Jan. 1, 1962–Dec. 31, 1964	4,500[3]	900[4]	3	1,500	300

[1] Dollar limit for appropriation to reimburse the Commodity Credit Corporation for cost of agricultural commodities shipped under Title I transactions, and authorized expenditures for Title II programs.

[2] Public Law 540, 84th Cong., approved May 28, 1956.

[3] Maximum of $2.5 billion during any one calendar year. Did not provide for carryover beyond Dec. 31, 1961, of unused balances from previous authorizations.

[4] $300 million each calendar year, plus carryover.

[5] Carryover of unused authorizations only.

SOURCE: This table is based on *Food for Peace—Nineteenth Semiannual Report on Public Law 480*, House Document No. 294–88/2, April 3, 1964, p. 9.

the Eighty-eighth Congress in 1964. Yet, Congressional behavior did not conform to this anticipation. A brief examination of other factors and variables involved in the pre-1964 extensions of the program will shed some light on the reasons behind the 1964 deviation.[1]

The 1957 extension of Public Law 480 for one year was surrounded by considerable disagreement as to the purposes of the Act. "Originally conceived as an agricultural program, Public Law 480's foreign policy aspects had assumed increasing importance and were subject to searching examination by Congress in 1957."[2] President Eisenhower's legislative request asked Congress to extend the program for only one year to increase Title I authorizations to $4 billion and to permit Public Law 480 barter with the communist countries of Eastern Europe. (This last item had been requested in 1956, but the House had refused to accept it.) As the following remarks of Ezra Taft Benson, then Secretary of Agriculture, indicate, the Eisenhower Administration did not want expansion of the program:

> Public Law 480 is considered a temporary means of disposal of agricultural surpluses. It has proved to be an effective tool of moving surpluses abroad while other programs are restoring a more balanced situation with respect to farm output and demand. However, sales for foreign currencies and barter are inconsistent with the Administration's foreign trade policy and with the Administration's desire to further the removal of Government from business. No action should be taken to incorporate disposal methods of this kind as permanent features of United States foreign trade program.[3]

The requested increase in Title I authorization and President Eisenhower's request for permission to barter with communist nations actually did not contradict Benson's views since both queries were aimed at a particular phenomenon rather than general expansion of the program. Following the October, 1956, Polish upheaval, the State Department, on December 26, announced that the "independent communist" regime of Wladyslaw Gomulka would be eligible for Public Law 480 sales. Consequently Eisenhower's request for increased authorization and expanded barter authority was intended to facilitate negotiations with the Polish government.

No longer a panacea

Congressional response to the request indicated that the early Congressional image of Public Law 480, as a panacea for the solution of domestic agricultural and foreign economic problems, had become somewhat tarnished. The Senate, accepting the Eisenhower request with satisfaction, made no efforts to expand the program. In the House of Representatives, many congressmen felt that even the Eisenhower request was far too much. The House Committee on Agriculture, for example, in reporting on the House bill, was "disturbed and alarmed" by the manner in which the administrators of Public Law 480 had interpreted the original legislation and by the failure of these administrators to place sufficient emphasis on use of the program for the development of foreign markets for United States agricultural products. A strong (and partially successful) effort was made on the floor of the House by Representatives Rooney (D-New York), Whitten (D-Mississippi), and other members of the Appropriations Committee to return control of Title I currencies to the Congress. There was, in addition, considerable debate on the floor of the House over the efficacy of granting Public Law 480 assistance to communist nations. Yet, a provision authorizing aid to such nations was contained in the final House bill. The conference committee agreed, however, to permit barter with East European communist nations and omitted House provisions restricting the use of foreign currencies. Title I authorization of the final bill was considerably less than the President had requested.

Additional Congressional dissatisfaction with the administration of Public Law 480 emerged during Senate Committee on Agriculture and Forestry hearings held the same year. The hearings were called for the purpose of overcoming the "failure of the public to be fully informed about the beneficial effects . . . of this program to the Departments of our Government other than the Department of Agriculture."[4] During the course of these hearings, the Assistant Secretary of Agriculture, Earl L. Butz, expressed the opinion that Public Law 480 was disrupting normal markets, while the Assistant Secretary of State, Thorsten V. Kalijarvi, stated that Public Law 480 had caused serious problems in United States relations with other exporting countries.

Thus it would seem that the dramatic reduction in Public Law 480 in 1957 was the result of two things: First, Executive worries over the side effects of the program, which mitigated any desire for expansion, and second, general Congressional disgruntlement over the implementation of Public Law 480.

Extension requested

On January 13, 1958, President Eisenhower asked the Congress to extend the program for another year and to increase Title I authorizations to $5.5 billion. This time Congressional response was milder.

While the Title I authorization ultimately approved was considerably short of what the Executive had requested, Congress had added six months to the extension. Congressional controversy was restricted to the barter aspect of the program—an issue instigated by State Department criticism which alleged that this aspect of the program was hurting United States foreign relations. No major modifications of the program were made by the Congress as a result of these discussions.

As discussed in Chapter II, the 1959 extension of Public Law 480 was surrounded by the complicated political maneuvering of three groups: (1) the Humphrey faction, which made a concentrated effort to strengthen the foreign policy aspects of Public Law 480 operations; (2) the Eisenhower Administration, which attempted to initiate a "Food for Peace" program without changing the temporary and surplus disposal aspects of Public Law 480; and (3) a group of congressmen who desired to restrict Public Law 480 objectives to the disposal of agricultural surpluses in as efficient a manner as was possible.

The 1959 Executive request, as presented by the President in his January 19 Budget Message to Congress, asked for a one-year extension of Titles I and II with authorizations of $1.5 billion and $300 million, respectively. Shortly thereafter, on January 29, the President launched his "Food for Peace" program under the direction of Secretary Benson. When the Administration's request was being considered before the House Agriculture Committee in July, Assistant Secretary of Agriculture, Clarence M. Miller, requested additional Public Law 480 amendments for the implementation of the new program. These proposals, however, dealt with expansion of the uses of Public Law 480 commodities and currencies rather than with the period of extension and authorizations.

The central issue in the House, as developed in the committee and carried to the floor, was "whether the Public Law 480 program should tend more toward donations and semidonations as a tool of foreign policy, or toward the exporting of agricultural surpluses on as nearly a business-like basis as possible."[5] The House committee, while expanding the barter provisions, reported out what was essentially an Administration bill. On the floor of the House, a new Title IV—authorizing long-term credit sales of surpluses for dollars—was added to the program, and provision was made for annual review of Title I currencies by the Appropriations Committees. Thus, the House bill reflected the view that it was possible to export surpluses on a business-like basis and, at the same time, expand food donations as an instrument of United States foreign policy.

In the Senate there was even greater concern expressed over the objectives of Public Law 480. Senator Humphrey's initial proposal of April 16, as referred to the Committee on Foreign Relations, would have extended Food-for-Peace operations even beyond their present scope. The Humphrey bill proposed a five-year extension of Titles I and II with an annual authorization of $2 billion and $250 million, respectively, the expansion of the barter program, the addition of a new Title IV, and a five-year program of surplus food donations to the less-developed nations for the purpose of building up food reserves. In hearings held by the Foreign Relations Committee, the Administration expressed strong opposition to the Humphrey proposals. The Deputy Assistant Secretary of State for Economic Affairs, W. T. M. Beale, commented on July 17 that the acceptance of such proposals would, "create false hopes and exaggerated expectations of economic aid on the part of recipient countries or would tend to result in over-programming of commodities in an attempt to meet these expectations."[6] Similar views were expressed by Clarence M. Miller, Assistant Secretary of Agriculture. The Humphrey bill came out of committee with serious modification but with a "do pass" recommendation.

In its initial consideration of the Executive request, the Senate Committee on Agriculture and Forestry reported out on July 15 a bill which conformed to Eisenhower's proposals. The committee, however, attached the proviso that this report was, "to be followed by consideration of needed amendments."[7] When the Senate committee resumed consideration of Public Law 480 legislation later in August, Senator Humphrey successfully proposed some of the provisions of his bill as amendments to the Agriculture Committee bill.

Give-away is feared

Although the proposed legislation considered on the floor of the Senate in early September fell far short of Humphrey's initial expectations, there was strong opposition to his added provisions to the original committee bill. Allen J. Ellender (D-Louisiana), Chairman of the Committee on Agriculture and Forestry, expressed opposition to the new three-year extension period which had been inserted into the committee bill, alleging that it would turn Public Law 480 "into a very definite arm of our foreign aid give-away program."[8] Senator Spessard L. Holland (D-Florida) stated that acceptance of the Humphrey amendments, "would be about as fatal a mistake in our protection of agriculture as we could make to commit ourselves in advance to the proposition that we are going to overproduce our commodities for the domestic and world markets."[9] Such opposition thus eliminated all of

Humphrey's amendments on the floor of the Senate with the exception of the three-year extension period, which was reduced to two years in the conference committee. This committee also approved a new Title IV provision as contained in the House bill and dropped the Administration's "Food for Peace" proposals, except for the provision authorizing the use of Title I currencies for emergency aid. Thus it would seem that the final product represented a compromise among the three groups. While neither Humphrey, the Executive, nor the group viewing Public Law 480 as essentially a surplus disposal program was successful in dominating the outcome of the 1959 extension, all had managed to incorporate some of their proposals into the new law. The overall result of the 1959 legislation was moderate expansion of the program and an increase in the use of Public Law 480 as an instrument of foreign policy.

While Public Law 480 was not amended by the Congress in 1960, there were three developments that affected the program during that year. On April 4, 1960, a special review committee appointed by the State Department and headed by Edward Mason submitted a report on the accumulation of Title I currencies. After numerous criticisms of the manner in which such currencies were being utilized, the Mason report urged that Public Law 480 be seriously conceived as a foreign aid program since it had outlived its usefulness as an instrument of surplus disposal. A second important development relating to Public Law 480 was the signing of the 1960 Indian Wheat Agreement on May 4—the largest single surplus food sale ever made by the United States. Apparently the Eisenhower Administration had decided to take advantage of the existing situation by utilizing surplus agricultural commodities for establishing friendships and cooperation with foreign countries. The Congress, forced to approve the sale against its wishes, responded with a protest voiced by many Congressmen and Senators. Typical of the general feelings of Congress was Whitten's criticism of the Administration for making surpluses a permanent feature of American agricultural policy, while disposing of them at 100 percent loss. Finally, an amendment to Public Law 480, contained in the Mutual Security Act of 1960, authorized food-for-wages projects under Title II, to free funds vitally needed for other development projects in the developing countries.

Economic development program

As soon as the Democratic Administration took office, President Kennedy appointed former Congressman George S. McGovern as director of a new Food for Peace. Under McGovern's leadership, Food for Peace became more and more an economic development program.

The Executive request for Public Law 480 extension in 1961 was part of the so-called omnibus farm bill. The Administration asked the Congress to extend Public Law 480 for five years and authorize $7.5 billion for Title I. Incorporation of the proposed Public Law 480 provisions into the Agricultural Act of 1961 was explained by Secretary Freeman as an effort to, "effectively tie the goals for American agriculture to the objective of United States foreign policy, with maximum gains for both."[10] Because of the complexity of the omnibus farm bill and the time allotted to Congress to process it, Public Law 480 received relatively little attention. In contrast to other extension periods, there were only scattered discussions on Public Law 480 in the Senate and House hearings, relatively few controversial issues, and very little consideration of this aspect of the bill on the floor of either house. In spite of the brief attention devoted to the Executive request, the Congress reduced the five-year period to three years, the $7.5 billion to $4.5 billion, and made several minor amendments to the program.

In 1961, two significant changes could be observed in the attitude of the Administration toward Public Law 480. First, the period of extension was raised to an unprecedented five years. Second, the Department of State, for the first time, came out in strong support for Public Law 480 as, "an important factor in the foreign relations of the United States."[11] Both changes were attributable to Democratic control of the Executive branch of the government.

In 1962, President Kennedy requested three amendments to Public Law 480 to strengthen Food for Peace. Two of these requests—to purchase surplus products not in federal stockpiles on the open market, and to donate food surpluses to international economic development programs—were rejected by Congress. The request to expand Title IV by permitting government-to-private-trade agreements, however, was accepted with only slight modification.

A provision contained in the Foreign Aid Bill of 1962 also lends insight into the issues of the 1964 extension and amendment of Public Law 480. Whereas the 1962 Foreign Aid Bill halted aid to communist nations, Public Law 480 was specifically excluded from this provision on the floor of the Senate and in the final law, thus permitting continuation of Public Law 480 program aid both to Poland and Yugoslavia.[12]

What generalizations can be derived from this survey of Congressional attitudes toward Public Law 480? The first and most important phenomenon was the recurrence of several unresolved issues in the Congress during nine years (1954-1962) of Public Law 480 operation. Most serious and frequently discussed issue in the Congress was whether the intent of Public Law 480 should be donations as a tool of foreign policy, or concessional sales of agricultural surpluses as part of domestic agricultural policy. Other issues included the question of long- or short-term program extensions, assistance to communist nations, the role of Congress in supervising program operations, accumulations of unused Title I proceeds, and the question of organizational efficiency to implement the program according to Congressional desires. These issues remained unresolved because of two intervening factors. The first was an uncooperative Republican Administration (1954-1960) and a restricted Democratic Congress. The second factor was a combination of successful attempts on the part of Eisenhower and Kennedy to confuse Congress by pre-empting Senator Humphrey's plans for revitalizing Public Law 480 and by burying Public Law 480 in the omnibus farm bill.

Until the 1958 Congressional elections, Public Law 480 suffered from the influence Eisenhower exerted on the Congress. However, once the Democratic margin had increased substantially in both houses of Congress, a new initiative to expand Public Law 480 was now in the making. With election of the Kennedy Administration and substantial Democratic control of the Congress, a new Food for Peace program and substantial expansion of Public Law 480 were realized. The issues, however, failed to be resolved, mostly because a Democratically controlled Congress had no interest in embarrassing a new Democratic Administration, and because there was no opportunity for the Congress to scrutinize the program until the new extension period in 1964.

Effect of Congressional image

How did the Congressional image of Public Law 480 affect the Executive attitude toward the program? During the Eisenhower Administration, Public Law 480 was viewed as a short-term, temporary program. There was, therefore, very little incentive to establish either an effective administrative apparatus or a mechanism for program evaluation. Although the Democratic Administration made several attempts to remedy these deficiencies, it was equally unsuccessful in satisfying Congressional expectations. The establishment of the Agency for International Development in 1961, with facilities for research and development, came too late to provide the needed index for Food for

Peace evaluation. At the same time, it generated in Congress a resentment which was reflected in the 1964 hearings and debates on Public Law 480.

CONGRESSIONAL DECISION MAKING

The foregoing evaluation of Congressional attitudes toward Public Law 480 is based on perceptions of expressions by various decision makers within the context of the legislative process. This process may be looked upon as the interaction between a superior and a subordinate system. Since Administrative request serves only as a stimulus to an authoritative response made by Congress, the decision-making power rests solely with that body. In the past there have been four occasions when the interaction between the two systems took place: 1957, 1958, 1959, and 1961. All four were years of extension of Public Law 480 programs. All four followed a process guided by comparable rules which not only provides continuity but systematization of the interaction. A close examination of these four extensions reveals how the systems operate.[13]

The Executive system is composed of units which interact in terms of inputs, outputs and feedback. There are two types of inputs in the Executive system: demands and supports. Demands are natural consequences of the desires of all participants in the program. On the one hand, there are external demands made by nongovernmental interest groups; on the other, there are internal demands voiced by the administrators of the program as a result of changes desired by different subgroups within the governmental organization of Public Law 480. Supports are endorsements of demands by the decision makers. In the Executive system, the decision makers are members of the Food for Peace Executive Committee who examine all demands and render their support for those they seek to promote and thus make recommendations to the President whose authoritative decision making determines the final content of the Executive request. When a demand —external or internal—gains support, it automatically becomes an issue. Hence the resolution of issues by the decision makers becomes the output of the Executive system. All outputs have a feedback which affects the future demands and support of the Executive system. Since the Executive system is part of the overall Public Law 480 decision-making process, the outputs of the Executive system (the Executive request) become one of several demands in the Congressional system.

Differences in two systems

Although the properties (inputs, outputs, feedbacks) of the Congressional system are the same as in the Executive system, the actors are different. In the Congressional system, external demands come from those permitted to testify before the hearings and informal lobbyists. Internal demands are generated by the decision makers as a result of their satisfaction or dissatisfaction with the program. Whereas, in the Executive system, the decision makers were top administrators directly involved in the program policy making under the President as the final arbiter, in the Congressional system the decision makers are all Congressmen and Senators as stratified by organizational rules, with the President holding the veto power. When these decision makers render their support for any demands, Congressional issues are produced which must ultimately be resolved either by acquiescence or rejection. Support and demand are not confined to any particular stage of the legislative process; they can originate in committees, in subcommittees, or on the floor. Whether a demand will receive Congressional support will depend not only on the quantity but also on the quality of those seeking to promote such a demand. A further condition determining support in the Congressional system is the way in which decisions are reached. There are both formal and informal rules of Congressional decision making. The outputs of the Congressional system (legislation sent to the President) create a feedback which influences both Congressional and Executive attitudes toward future Public Law 480 decision making.

What emerges from this survey of attitudes and processes reflecting the Congressional image of Public Law 480 is the indication that by 1964, there were certain identifiable patterns of executive-legislative behavior, which enable a systematic analysis of the politics of Food for Peace during an extension period. The last extension of Public Law 480 in 1964 is such a case. Since our objective is to examine the politics of Food for Peace as reflected in Congressional decision making during 1964, the main focus of this study will be on the executive-legislative interaction during the extension period. This can be accomplished first by analyzing the formulation of the 1964 Executive request, and second, by the analysis of the Congressional response. The latter task has two parts: (1) examination of Congressional arguments waged in the Congress, as reflected in terms of issues surrounding the 1964 extension, and (2) the voting behavior of Congressional decision makers.

Chapter 4

The Executive Request: Unity and Conflict

THE EXECUTIVE'S POSITION vis-à-vis the 1964 extension and amendment was formally presented to the Congress in the form of a letter, February 18, 1964, from Secretary Freeman to the President pro tem of the Senate and the Speaker of the House of Representatives. The specific issues were as follows:[1]

It is proposed that the authority to enter into agreements under Title I be extended five calendar years through December 31, 1969, and increased by $7.1 billion for the five-year period with a limitation of $2.5 billion for any calendar year with provision for the carry-over of uncommitted authorizations from prior years; the use of foreign currencies be authorized for procurement of equipment, materials, facilities, and services for internal security programs, in addition to the military categories presently authorized for the common defense; the existing 25 percent limitation on loans to private business firms be eliminated; authorization be included for the sale of Title I currencies for dollars to voluntary agencies and to United States flag vessels for payment of certain expenses incurred under the act; the requirement of reports on activities under the act be changed from every six months to each year and the Title II authority be increased to $450 million for each of the calendar years 1965 through 1969 and authority to make general average contributions be extended to Title III and related shipments.

EXECUTIVE STRATEGY

Since Executive Order 10900 delegated to USDA the primary responsibility for administration and implementation of Public Law 480 programs, it was the Secretary of Agriculture who introduced the legislative request on behalf of the Executive. This is not to imply, however, that the ten proposals as listed reflected solely the interests of USDA. The converse, in fact, was the case. A close scrutiny of the proposals reveals that all ten, including the request for a five-year

67

extension of Titles I and II, reflect increasing emphasis upon the foreign aid operations of Public Law 480. As pointed out in Chapter II, in spite of extensive delegations of Public Law 480 authority to USDA, most of the foreign operations of the program fall within the purview of AID. It is, reasonable, therefore, to assume that while AID was acting in the role of the proponent, USDA was willing to endorse AID's requests. The Executive proposals concerning periods of extension, and the authorization of funds for Title I and II, clearly indicate desire to make the programs more effective as instruments of foreign policy by permitting long-term foreign aid planning which would produce more confidence in the recipients. These proposals would have automatically done away with the "Congressional minuet" involving long arduous preparation for legislative rituals and short periods for administrative duties. The Executive also asked Congress to authorize the use of Title I currencies for internal security programs and to increase the amount of such currencies available for loans to private enterprise in recipient countries; these proposals reflected a desire to use accumulated Title I currencies for development purposes within recipient countries. The Executive's proposals for sale of Title I currencies to voluntary agencies and to United States flag vessels were intended to increase utilization of accumulations of foreign currencies thereby facilitating shipment and distribution of Food for Peace commodities. The request for authorization of payment of general average contributions for Title III shipments may also be construed as directed at more efficient distribution and transportation of commodities. The final request of the Executive for a reduction in the frequency of Presidential reporting apparently aimed to expand the time element so that progress could be gauged with greater accuracy.

STRATEGY FORMULATION

Examination of the formulation of these proposals further clarifies the prevailing role of AID in the decision-making process. The final Executive request was the result of a variety of proposals for Public Law 480 legislation submitted by government agencies, voluntary groups, and individuals interested in the Food for Peace program during the latter part of 1963. Three among these were of direct significance. On December 26, Secretary Freeman chaired a meeting of Agriculture, AID, and Food for Peace people to establish the general strategy outlines. This was followed by a Freeman-Reuter luncheon to continue these discussions on December 31. As a result, proposals and specific comments were drawn up by two working committees: one from the Department of Agriculture, and a second from AID. Voluntary agencies also submitted suggestions, at AID request, through the Council of Voluntary Agencies for Foreign Service, as did farm groups, trade groups, members of Mr. O'Brien's staff, interested congressmen, and citizen advisors. The Food for Peace staff then coordinated suggestions of the various groups and agencies to be presented in a checklist for discussion by the Food for Peace Executive Committee in a meeting on January 21, 1964. Participants discussed the proposals[2] in the checklist and made recommendations for the 1964 extension and amendment of Public Law 480. The gist of the recommendations was incorporated ten days later by President Johnson in his farm message to the Congress,[3] which provided the base for Secretary Freeman's formal presentation of the Executive request to Congress.

Analysis of documents

A comparative analysis of three documents—the Food for Peace staff checklist, recommendations by the Food for Peace Executive Committee, and Secretary Freeman's letter to Congress—reveals the preeminent role of AID in molding the final draft of the Executive proposal. Six of the ten Executive proposals were in complete accord with recommendations by the Food for Peace Executive Committee. The remaining four—use of Title I currencies for internal security programs in recipient countries, sale of Title I currencies to United States flag vessels, sale of Title I currencies to voluntary agencies, and general average contributions for Title III—were in no way inimical to the interests of AID. Of the proposals which were not incorporated into the Food for Peace Executive Committee recommendations nor into Secretary Freeman's letter, all seven can be interpreted as being objectionable to AID. These suggestions are: (1) omission of the word "surplus" from the preamble of Public Law 480 which could have been interpreted by AID as the removal of a useful facade which facilitated the use of Public Law 480 as an instrument of United States foreign policy; (2) provision of short-term credit concessional sales of CCC commodities for noncommercial use to assist the extension of school lunch and institutional programs under host country initiative which was conceived by AID as an unbusinesslike form of sale because it could not be justified in terms of world market prices; (3) the provision that five percent of Title I purchase prices could be specified in third country currency for the use of the United States, which AID opposed because of the potential foreign exchange loss from such a proposal; (4) the authorization of expansion of the use of market development (Section 104a) local currency funds for other trade expansion purposes which would have provided a drain on the supply of foreign currencies available for AID development purposes; (5) the use of AID appropriated funds for the expansion of food distribution programs in recipient countries which would have reduced the funds available for other Public Law 480 AID programs; (6) use of local currencies to provide necessary capital expenditures for host governments and voluntary agencies engaged in food distribution programs (opposed by AID as competitive with its own Public Law 480 programs); and (7) granting of greater flexibility to the CCC for processing as necessary to insure nutritional or market development goals (probably opposed by AID because of interdepartmental jealousy and fear that the CCC may encroach upon AID's domain). On the basis of this evidence it would be fair to conclude, however, that any disagreements concerning the formulation of the final Executive request were mild in contrast to Congressional response. None of the differences were aired in public or required the assistance of arbitration by higher authority.

THE ROLE OF AID

A possible key to AID's position of leadership in the formulation of the Executive request may be found in the history of the development of Public Law 480. After 1956, the State Department and its foreign aid agency (International Cooperation Administration and its successor, AID) began to view Public Law 480 programs as a viable instrument of foreign policy. Gradually, ICA and AID, under the shield of surplus disposal, made Public Law 480 and Food for Peace what the late President Kennedy described as the programs ". . . increasingly using our agricultural commodities to stimulate the economic growth of developing nations and to assist in achieving other United States foreign policy goals."[4] Two things emerge from this trend. The first is that Public Law 480 was passed originally as a domestic program for the disposal of agricultural surpluses with only peripheral foreign aid objectives. Many provisions were, therefore, included in the law which later became antithetical to the overall foreign policy objectives of the United States. Because of the broad allowance for administrative discretion in the original law, the State

Department and its agencies took the initiative and transformed the operation of Public Law 480 programs into an instrument of foreign aid. Second, as a result, AID did not hesitate to pay lip service to the intent of the law while at the same time instigating changes to reduce the inherent contradictions involved in using a surplus disposal program for foreign aid purposes.

Issues unresolved

In spite of piecemeal success, AID did not succeed in resolving the basic issue whether Public Law 480 and, consequently, Food for Peace, could simultaneously satisfy the domestic and foreign interests in the programs. Hence, certain conflicts in the operations of the Food for Peace program have been noticeable throughout its history. For example, George McGovern, a former director of Food for Peace, observed that the program was ". . . heavily burdened with interagency delay, bureaucratic timidity and Executive branch fears of Congressional reaction."[5]

In the absence of clearly defined purposes and objectives in Public Law 480, participating agencies have shown a tendency to define the program in terms of differing self-interests. For example, the USDA's conception of the program is directed toward domestic agricultural interests, the State Department is primarily influenced by its concern with United States foreign relations. AID, on the other hand, is more concerned with economic development abroad and less with its impact on United States foreign and domestic policies. The White House Office of Food for Peace views Public Law 480 as a catalyst serving interests both humanitarian and domestic. The two key mechanisms for the resolution of these varying perceptions are the Interagency Staff Committee (ISC), as discussed in Chapter II, and the Food for Peace Policy Committee. The latter—composed of members of the involved agencies at the Assistant Secretary level—was established in October, 1962, by the director of Food for Peace, apparently in an effort to restore among the participating agencies the balance of decision-making power which was supposed to exist in the ISC. The effectiveness of ISC, as a body coordinating the development and review of programs, operations and basic agreements negotiated under Title I, was seemingly hampered by the dual and possibly conflicting role of AID. It has been alleged,[6] for example, that AID represents the Department of State as well as itself, at ISC meetings and has the Presidential authority to waive the Congressional appropriation requirement in the case of outright grants of foreign currency. In Senator McGee's own words:

> It would seem, therefore, that AID, in its quite dominant position as principal member of the interagency committee which determines how the sales proceeds will be used, and is the chief user of these funds, is acting in the role of both judge and jury. This would seem to be even more true in the case of its present delegated Presidential authority of waiving congressional appropriation requirements in the case of outright grants. There would seem to be a conflict of interest between its role as chief user of the funds and its role of determining what percentage of the total proceeds from the sales would be allocated for its use—even between the purposes of which grant funds are to be used, economic assistance, or common defense.[7]

Granted the validity of this allegation, AID has consistently defended its dominant position as necessary, due to lack of coordination in planning foreign assistance programs and to being charged with the responsibility for success of the increasingly foreign aid-tinged character of the program. This interpretation gained recognition and acceptance not only in Congress, but also in USDA. For instance, Secretary Freeman's reply to Senator Young is a case in point:

> SENATOR YOUNG: What part of this program would you say is of direct benefit to agriculture and what part would be a part of our foreign aid program? Have you ever figured that out?
> SECRETARY FREEMAN: Well, I would decline to assess a percentage value to it, Senator Young. It accomplishes that and other goals as well. . . . It is important as a part of our foreign policy as it seeks to strengthen and assist some of the developing countries to maintain their course in the direction of freedom. And certainly it dramatizes as nothing else does the superiority of American free enterprise family farm system over the collectivized Communist agriculture. . . . And I think that one of the overwhelming parts of this program that has made it such a success, and I say this advisedly, is that I think it will go down as one of the most outstanding things done in the history of mankind, is because it does have this multiple effect of serving the mutual interests of so many people.[8]

Another possible conflict in the decision-making process of the Food for Peace program, where the differing perceptions of participating agencies become apparent, may arise when concessional sales of surplus commodities interfere with normal commercial trading. There have been cases in the past when recommendations by USDA have been overruled by the Department of State because they did not conform to the Department's policies.[9] There have also been cases when cooperation between AID, the State Department and USDA has been strained as the result of Food for Peace transactions which interfered with the normal commercial sales by nations friendly to the United States: for example, Canada, Australia, Argentina, New Zealand, etc. Furthermore, Food for Peace sales may have become a source of friction among the participating agencies due to the tendency of such sales to depress world market prices. Still another source of conflict among the Executive members of the program is possible when food aid interferes with the normal agricultural production of the recipient nations and thus may create disagreement between AID and USDA.

EXECUTIVE TACTICS

Once the Executive request was formulated, all Executive agencies involved in the operation of the Food for Peace program had no alternative but to unite behind the proposal for the sake of furthering their own interests. Thus united, the Executive agencies followed tactics outlined by the Executive Committee Meeting on January 21, 1964. It was felt that since Congress would be under pressure to move rapidly with respect to the extension and amendment of Public Law 480, it would be advisable to request a simple extension of existing legislation with relatively few amendments. This optimistic outlook toward Congressional response now appears unrealistic in the light of certain events preceding formulation of the Executive request. There were several criticisms contained in documents presented in the latter part of 1963. For example:[10] (1) The Foreign Assistance (authorization) Act, which placed restrictions on Public Law 480 sales to aggressor nations, revised Title I exchange rates, expanded provisions for use of Title I currencies, and authorized Executive study groups; (2) a report by Senator Gruening (D-Alaska) which criticized Public Law 480 sales to the United Arab Republic on the grounds that ". . . to the extent we relieve Nasser's normal budget of the cost of food and fibre . . . he can divert that much into his arms budget;" (3) a report by Senator Gale McGee (D-Wyoming) which was submitted to the Senate Appropriations Committee; this report pointed out that AID should do "a great deal more" to realize "the full potential" of Public Law 480 programs and was especially critical of the utilization of Title I currencies; (4) the House Subcommittee on Information and Foreign Operations held hearings during which existing use of Title I foreign currencies was questioned. One can assume that these criticisms were strong enough to provide the Executive agencies with a preview of Congressional attitudes toward the program. Thus it is legitimate to entertain the question of whether or not the Executive agencies took advantage of these "warning signals."

Tactics examined

As an examination of the House hearings (which began on February 18) reveals, the tactics of the Executive agencies seemed evasive, obfuscating, and loquacious. Four guidelines seem to have been employed by the Executive agencies in defense of their legislative request:[11] (1) The thrust of Executive arguments for extension and amendment urged continuation of the program because of the domestic agricultural and market interests which the program served; (2) the burden of defending the Executive position thus fell to USDA which not only had most of the delegated responsibility for administration of Title I, but also was in the best position to present documentary evidence to Congress on this particular aspect; (3) there was an attempt to answer pointed Congressional questions in an oblique manner by passing the responsibility from one agency to another; (4) rather than justifying their request item by item, representatives of the Executive—with a few exceptions—adopted a defensive posture urging Congress to approve the Executive proposal as a package deal. The rationale for such tactics becomes apparent when one considers the handicap under which the Executive agencies were operating during the legislative process. The Executive, not possessing any evaluative documentation of the entire Food for Peace program, could not prepare briefs supporting itemized requests with tangible evidence and had no alternative but to be fatalistic as to the Congressional response. Obviously, then, the Executive was in no position to make use of the "warning signals" flashing Congressional dissatisfaction with certain aspects of the program. Therefore, it would be an oversimplification to accuse the Executive of overoptimism in its anticipation of success and of naïveté about Congressional scrutiny.

SUMMARY

The foregoing analysis shows that intra-Executive disagreements on formulation of the Executive request and operation of the programs can occur most frequently within the context of specific cases related to the Food for Peace policy, whereas disagreements on formulation of legislative requests occur only at specified intervals. Both of these major areas are derived from inherent contradictions between Food for Peace and Public Law 480 as discussed in Chapter 2. The clash of domestic versus foreign policy interests arises from statutory differences in missions and mandates.[12] With time and expansion of the program this problem has increased in severity. In spite of the handicap created by this problem, the program has been able to function effectively amid considerable amity and understanding among participating agencies in the Executive branch of the government. Nevertheless, sources of friction are present and constitute a threat to the long future of the program. A good example of this threat is the arbitration of unresolved decisions concerning Title I and IV sales. Although the Director of AID, David E. Bell, stated before Congressional hearings in 1964 that ". . . if any of us wished to take [Secretary Freeman] to the President we may, but that has not happened in the period I have been there."[13] Yet, in early 1966, the final decision on Title I agreement with India was left for the President to decide. Thus what appeared on the surface to be a unified Executive request for legislation, submitted to the Congress on February 18, 1964, was in reality a product of diverse interests united in an effort to face Congress. The tactics used by the Executive agencies are further evidence in support of this conclusion. As the Congressional committee hearings revealed, once the facade was penetrated by Congressional scrutiny, cracks in the wall of Executive unity could be discerned.

Chapter 5

The Congressional Response: Issues and Arguments

THE EXECUTIVE REQUEST for Public Law 480 legislation for 1964 immediately stimulated both support and opposition in Congress, and there was some neutrality as well. As soon as Congressional debate was formalized, the attitudes of members of Congress began to crystalize around specific issues. The first type of issue arose from Executive request, while the second type was derived from Congressional scrutiny and had support in at least one decisional unit of the Congress. Since both types of issues were decided by the Congress alone —the President having no practical alternative but to accept the decision—it can be argued that the Congress acted here as both judge and jury.

Although Congressional decision making may give the impression of being monolithic in nature, in reality the legislative process is complex, dynamic, and decentralized. It involves many decisional units interacting in a cumulative fashion permitting the introduction and examination of new issues while responding to an initial stimulus. Five such units of the Eighty-eighth Congress constituted the decision-making system which extended and amended Public Law 480 in 1964. These units were: (1) the House Committee on Agriculture, (2) the Senate Committee on Agriculture and Forestry, (3) the floor of the House of Representatives, (4) the floor of the Senate, and (5) the conference committee. Our task in this chapter will be to trace responses to the Executive request among Congressional decision makers within each of the component units.

THE HOUSE COMMITTEE ON AGRICULTURE

The House Committee on Agriculture assists the House of Representatives as a standing committee on legislation dealing with agriculture in general. In 1964, the House Committee on Agriculture was organized into eight standing subcommittees designed to consider

77

legislation relating to specific types of agricultural commodities, and into seven special subcommittees designed to act upon legislation comprising miscellaneous agricultural interests. Because of the volume of business relating to agriculture, the size of the committee (thirty-five members in 1964), and the complexity of agricultural legislation calling for special skill and expert knowledge, the groundwork for committee decisions is assigned to the various subcommittees. Such was the case in the House Committee on Agriculture with regard to the extension and amendment of Public Law 480.

Assigned to handle this matter was the Subcommittee on Foreign Agricultural Operations, established in 1954 especially to consider matters relating to Public Law 480. In response to Executive request, the group held four days of hearings on the "Extension of Public Law 480—Titles I and II," met in executive session to "mark up" the bill and make recommendations to the full committee, wrote the committee report to the House, defended the committee bill on the floor, and participated in the conference committee. The regular members of the subcommittee were six Democrats and four Republicans. The chairman was the veteran Congressman, W. R. Poage (D-Texas). The chairman of the full committee, Harold D. Cooley (D-North Carolina), as well as the ranking minority leader of the full committee, Charles B. Hoeven (R-Iowa), along with Albert H. Quie (R-Minnesota) and Paul Findley (R-Illinois), actively participated in the subcommittee hearings under House rules. In addition, one Republican and five Democrats from the full committee were also present during the hearings.

Two of the four days of subcommittee hearings (February 18 and 28) which produced 188 pages of testimony, provide a sample of Congressional attitudes toward the Executive request. As soon as Secretary Freeman had delivered his prepared statement on February 18, subcommittee Chairman Poage fired a barrage of questions challenging Public Law 480 operations. Chairman Poage's first criticism was directed at Title I currency grants, which he contended were suppressing world market prices for agricultural commodities. Poage's indictment was affirmed by Representative Jones (D-Missouri) who maintained that the indiscriminate use of grants and loans under Title I had resulted in our being made ". . . patsies in many of these countries." This criticism was lauded by Chairman Cooley. Jones also criticized the lack of observable political returns from such loans and grants, adding "I am not in favor of extending any kind of help, either through the sale, or gift, or anything else, . . . to people who do not feel some commitment to the United States of America and the tax-payers who are footing the bill."[1] Although Secretary Freeman yielded to some of these general allegations, he urged Congress to consider the ramifications surrounding decisions to make Title I grants.

> . . . We need to go to each of these programs on a country-by-country basis in connection with the economics of that country, of its agriculture, of its needs and also the overall political situation with regard to that country at a given time and place. All of these factors enter into it.
>
> I would only say that we seek to eliminate grants, other things being equal.[2]

A new issue was introduced when Congressman Hoeven asked Freeman, "Why do you want the five-year program?" Freeman's response and Hoeven's rebuttal are of interest:

> SECRETARY FREEMAN: Basically because we have found in these programs that a leadtime in connection with them is really quite important, because they do involve the implementing of programs that take some period of time, and the three-year period, while it was a period under which we think we operated effectively, a five-year period would make for greater continuity of planning and operation than we could on this other basis.
>
> MR. HOEVEN: I share the concern expressed by Chairman Poage and Mr. Jones and Mr. McIntire regarding some phases of this program. I believe Congress should have the opportunity to review the entire program periodically without extending the life for a longer time. I am not convinced that there should be a five-year extension.[3]

This exchange was followed by an extended discussion of the requested annual authorization for Title II of the program which was led by Representative Hoeven. Implicit in Hoeven's criticism was the allegation that Title II funds bypassed the Appropriations Committee and was therefore a "back-door spending program." Representatives Quie and Findley joined Hoeven in this charge. This assertion was strongly denied by Secretary Freeman who, for the first time, received support from Poage who observed:

> As I see this under Public Law 480, the Congress made the appropriation to the Commodity Credit Corporation to purchase these commodities. It is not back door spending there, because the Appropriations Committee appropriates whatever money is necessary to provide the capital stock for the Commodity Credit

Corporation. Congress authorizes that, and this committee is the one that authorizes the purchase of these commodities by the Commodity Credit Corporation. Having purchased the commodities it seems to me that there is no further question of legislative appropriation.[4]

A third and final issue, introduced on the first day of hearings, was Congressman Findley's proposal to make mandatory sales of Title I currencies to United States tourists in communist countries. Whereas Findley emphasized the excess currencies in Yugoslavia as a potential source of alleviation for United States gold outflow problems, he was, in reality, laying groundwork for a criticism of Public Law 480 sales to communist nations. Secretary Freeman, cognizant of the real issue, refused to engage in open confrontation with Congressman Findley and therefore restricted his comments to Findley's proposal to make such a provision mandatory. Obviously, then, the attempt by Findley (as the spokesman for the minority party) to embarrass both the Administration and the majority party failed during the first day of the hearings. However, his later attempt to bar Title I and IV Public Law 480 sales to communist nations met with success on the floor of the House.

A survey of the first day of hearings indicated that the three issues raised by the Subcommittee on Foreign Agricultural Operations—Title I grants, period of extension, and mandatory sales of Title I currencies to United States tourists—had a common denominator: the criticism of the foreign aid aspects of Public Law 480 operations. In view of the conclusions presented in Chapter IV, it can be deduced that Congressional subcommittee criticism was actually directed toward the role of AID in Public Law 480 operations. This becomes evident from the remarks of three leading members of the subcommittee during the first two days of hearings. Representatives Jones, McIntire, and Poage expressed a common concern over the interagency relationships in the decision-making process of Food for Peace. Chairman Poage, for example, offered the following observation:

> One of our greatest problems here, Mr. Derwinski, is that we do not know who to deal with in regard to this (matter of Title I currencies). Of course, theoretically we deal with the Department of Agriculture. We know perfectly well that the Department of Agriculture is not in on a great deal of these operations.[5]

The concern of the subcommittee over the role of the State Department in Public Law 480 programs was further aggravated by Freeman's hesitancy to resolve a problem created by Congress in 1954. Secretary Freeman's statement is self-explanatory:

> Let me answer that by saying that it is, I think, impossible to split off a part of this program which I believe strongly ought to be administered in the last analysis in close cooperation, but nonetheless ought to be administered by the Department of Agriculture.[6]

In addition to Secretary Freeman's testimony before the subcommittee, spokesmen for two other Executive agencies gave testimony in support of the Executive request. W. Averell Harriman, Undersecretary of State, and David E. Bell, Administrator of AID, appeared at the same time on February 28 to deliver prepared statements and answer questions posed by the subcommittee members. Having learned a lesson from the first day of the hearings, both Bell and Harriman selected and divided between themselves two out of the three issues raised by the subcommittee and exploited their advantage by presenting in their prepared statements a defense both of aid to communist nations and of Title I currency grants. Most of Harriman's presentation was devoted to the relationship between Food for Peace and communism. After emphasizing benefits derived by the United States from the contrast between American and communist agriculture, Harriman defended the impact of the Food for Peace program on Poland and Yugoslavia. Bell, on the other hand, stressed the domestic assets of the program. Public Law 480, according to Bell, made a vital contribution not only to the economic development of the less-developed nations of the Free World, but also to the American national interest by building security and agricultural export markets. Director Bell went as far as to claim that "Public Law 480 is basically an agricultural program."[7] With respect to the granting of Title I currencies, he noted:

> As the committee knows, we have over the last year or so limited very sharply the use of the grant authority and we will continue to do so.
>
> I also want to be frank in stating, however, that there are two countries, India and Pakistan, where we believe it is likely to prove in the best interests of the objectives of Public Law 480 to depart from the general policy of limiting grants when we face the necessity for renewing sales agreements with these countries.[8]

Whereas Undersecretary Harriman's prepared statement contained a one-sentence endorsement of the five-year extension period, Administrator Bell made no reference to this issue in his statement. The omission was quickly picked up by Congressman Hoeven, who expressed his opposition to the five-year extension because he felt the program needed periodic Congressional review. When Bell and Harriman made an attempt to defend the five-year extension period, Hoeven did not hesitate to remind them that ". . . the Committee on Agriculture is rather jealous of its rights and prerogatives" to which Bell replied, "I am sure that it is, Sir."[9]

A second issue dealt with Public Law 480 assistance to Yugoslavia. Congressman Poage questioned Director Bell on the manner in which excess Title I currencies had been used for the reconstruction of Skopje, after the 1963 earthquake. Representatives Cooley and Hoeven joined in the criticism and accused the Administration of failure to handle the situation in Yugoslavia swiftly and effectively. Later on, Congressman Harvey (R-Indiana) questioned Harriman's assertion that Yugoslavia had moved closer to the West because of Public Law 480 aid. Harvey was joined by Hoeven who was critical of Yugoslavia for its voting record in the United Nations. Harriman's reply to this charge is worth noting:

> Certainly, Yugoslavia is closer to Moscow today than she was a few years ago, but the change has been in Moscow, not in Yugoslavia. That is the important factor in this situation. The relationship of Moscow with all of the countries of Eastern Europe has been more in the direction of independence and it is for that reason that better relations have been able to be developed, on Yugoslavia's not on Moscow's terms.[10]

Third issue raised

Title I currency grants were a third issue raised by the subcommittee during the last day of hearings. As he did with Secretary Freeman, Chairman Poage opened the questioning of Harriman and Bell on this issue. Again, Poage's major concern was the adverse impact which such grants had on world market prices of agricultural commodities. Director Bell, who chose to answer Poage's question, argued that AID's Title I responsibilities were in programming and implementation, whereas USDA was responsible for preventing such transactions from suppressing world prices. Dissatisfied with Bell's explanation, Poage continued to probe the same problem, which covers nine pages of the record. He was not satisfied with the answers.

The nexus of the three issues above appears to be identical with that of the first day of hearings—the role of the Department of State and AID in what the committee members considered to be a program directed primarily toward domestic agricultural benefits. When both Harriman and Bell were pressed for direct answers (to indirect questions), they avoided this basic issue as best they could. With respect to the requested five-year period of extension of the program, Harriman politely deferred the justification for the request to the Secretary of Agriculture who ". . . is in a better position to explain . . . why the longer period is important to the program."[11] In defending Public Law 480 assistance to Yugoslavia, Harriman again deferred the decision to the National Security Council. Finally, with respect to Title I currency grants, Bell argued that the Secretary of Agriculture was primarily responsible for such grants.

Since one of the purposes of committee hearings is to "smoke out" the differences of opinions among interested parties, the Subcommittee on Foreign Agricultural Operations invited representatives of twenty-six interest groups to testify before the subcommittee during the last three days. This testimony was evenly divided with thirteen voluntary agencies as well as thirteen farm and business groups being represented. Among the voluntary agencies, only Paul C. Empie of the National Lutheran Council was in any way critical of the program. While generally supporting the Executive's request, Empie expressed concern over the expanding role of the voluntary agencies in the Food for Peace program. With this minor exception, the testimony of the representatives of the voluntary agencies strongly supported the five-year extension requested by the Executive—some agencies even expressing a desire to make the program permanent. There was scattered support for the general average contributions provision of the Executive request and some reference by voluntary agencies to other items specified by the Freeman letter. Of the ninety-seven farm and business groups, all but four expressed support for the Executive request (in the same general terms as did the voluntary agencies). However, the only major farm organization which supported the Executive request was the National Farmers Union; the remainder of the supporting faction consisted of agricultural commodity groups (except for the AFL-CIO). The four opposing groups submitted the following criticisms of the program.[12] The Chamber of Commerce urged the abolition of Public Law 480 and its replacement with a program in which: (1) funds for food aid would be appropriated by Congress, (2) food aid would be distributed on the basis of the needs of the recipient nations, and (3) the necessary commodities for such aid would be purchased by the federal government on the domestic market at market prices. The National Cotton Council recommended that the program be subjected to "critical review" and, wherever possible, that dollars be substituted for currencies. The National Grange, while supporting the five-year period of extension and other requests, expressed reservations about the use of proceeds in such a manner as to develop competition with American agriculture. Finally, John C. Lynn of the Farm Bureau urged that the period of extension for Titles I and II be limited to three years, and that the committee stipulate that at least 25 percent of Title I sales be in convertible currencies.

Introduction of H.R. 12298

The next aspect of the Congressional response, as reflected by the House Committee on Agriculture, began with the introduction of H.R. 12298 on August 7 by Representative Poage.[13] It is abundantly clear that this bill was shaped by the subcommittee's earlier hearings. The bill dealt with only three issues raised in the Executive request: the removal of the 25 percent limitation on Cooley loans; the approval of Title I currencies for internal security programs; and the extension and authorization for Titles I and II. The former two issues were incorporated by the Poage bill without change; the provision dealing with the period of extension and amount of authorization, however, differed significantly from the Executive request. Titles I and II were extended for only three years, with an authorization of approximately $1.7 billion per year for Title I and $450 million annually for Title II. In accordance with the charge of back-door spending leveled at Title I, the amount of foreign currencies subjected to the appropriations process was increased from 10 to 20 percent. The strong criticism voiced by congressmen in the committee produced a stipulation in the bill establishing a top-level, executive-legislative committee to advise the President on currency uses; Title I grants were made subject to the approval of this committee. Several other provisions for expansion of Title I currency uses were included also.

It is clear that Representative Poage had made every effort to incorporate into his bill the wishes of his colleagues for, when the bill was reported out of the Committee on Agriculture with a "do pass" recommendation, on August 11, it was unchanged except for the deletion of two minor provisions for Title I currency use.[14] Accompanying the House bill were two committee reports, those of the majority and minority factions. The majority report, submitted by Chairman Cooley and written by the subcommittee, was an explanation and justification of the committee bill. The minority report, on the other hand, contained bitter criticism of the program. It was written by Congressman Findley whose emotional style combined with personal observations irritated many of his colleagues. Findley's description of the program is a case in point:

> Public Law 480 is an example of a good idea gone astray. One reason—perhaps the principal one—is the complex nature of the program. Sam Lubell, who once called farm legislation a "conspiracy against public understanding," could very well have had Public Law 480 in mind as the prize exhibit to prove his contention.[15]

H.R. 12298, as reported out of committee, can be reasonably considered a victory for the Administration in spite of the criticism waged against the program by both factions of the House Committee on Agriculture. This view is supported by Secretary Freeman in his comments on the House bill during the Senate hearings on August 12, 1964.[16]

THE SENATE COMMITTEE ON AGRICULTURE AND FORESTRY

With few exceptions, the Senate follows the lead of its committees in accepting or rejecting legislation on the floor. Thus response to the Executive request of the Senate Committee on Agriculture and Forestry is of great importance. Although the Committee on Agriculture and Forestry had four standing subcommittees and one special subcommittee in 1964, none of these subcommittees were designed specifically for Public Law 480 legislation as in the case of the House. Consideration of the 1964 extension and amendment, therefore, was undertaken by the full Senate committee.

As organized in 1964, the Committee on Agriculture and Forestry had seventeen members—eleven Democrats and six Republicans. Only twelve senators, however, were present for the single day of committee hearings on August 12. Those being absent were: Spessard L. Holland (D-Florida), James O. Eastland (D-Mississippi), Bourke B. Hickenlooper (R-Iowa), and J. Caleb Boggs (R-Delaware). The chairman of the committee was the influential Allen J. Ellender (D-Louisiana).

Unlike the House, where committee hearings took the form of a direct Congressional response to the Executive request, the Senate hearings were directed toward a specific bill which had been introduced and referred to the Senate Committee on Agriculture and Forestry. One would expect, therefore, that the 107 pages of documents, testimony, and discussion produced by the Senate hearings would have been more succinct and more to the point than was actually the case.

Although the Senate bill (S. 2687) was introduced by Senator Ellender on March 25, committee hearings were not scheduled until August 12. While this bill contained all the provisions of the Executive request, it added four new items and, therefore, may not be considered as strictly an Administration bill. The four new provisions were: (1) limitation of ocean freight charges to the differential resulting from the Cargo Preference Act, (2) a stipulation that foreign currencies under Title I must be convertible to the extent consistent with the purposes of the act, (3) specification of minimum interest rates for Title I and IV loans, and (4) a provision which required that the proposed annual Presidential reports include an estimate of the real values of foreign currencies and a justification of exchange rates specified in agreements negotiated during the prior year.[17]

Secretary Freeman, while accompanied by Bell, presented the only prepared statement on behalf of the Administration. Harriman was not present. As he had in the House, Freeman chose to discuss the program in very general terms. He anticipated strong opposition from the chairman of the committee and, hence, adopted a conciliatory position.

Questions by Ellender

The rapid-fire nature of Ellender's questions is indicative that he knew what he wanted in the bill when it was reported out of his committee. Ellender, in his first question, asked Freeman to choose between a proposal subjecting all Title I currency expenditures to the appropriations process and the advisory committee proposed by the House bill which he had previously discussed with House members. Freeman refused to be pinned down and, therefore, chose a third and existing alternative. "I think the mechanism as it exists in the present law ought to be continued."[18]

Next, Ellender asked Freeman what he thought about the specification of minimum interest rates for Titles I and IV. Freeman saw no problem with respect to Title I programs but expressed opposition to such specification with respect to Title IV because of the inflexibility in programming which could be created.[19]

Without further examination of this matter, Chairman Ellender switched to another problem. First he expressed his dissatisfaction with the existing practice of saddling agriculture with the costs of the program, and then he proposed to charge the costs of the operation of the program to foreign aid. Senator Johnston (D-South Carolina) echoed Ellender's charge. However, neither Freeman nor Bell took issue with the two highest ranking members of the committee. Ellender continued to question Freeman and Bell until he was interrupted by Senator McGovern (D-South Dakota) who came to Freeman's defense. McGovern, as a tactical maneuver, changed the subject when Ellender cautioned Freeman ". . . do not let these boys from the State Department override you, because if they do, somebody is going to have to account to Congress for it . . ."[20] by asking Freeman to comment on the costs and benefits of the program to the American farmer and to the Department of Agriculture. This attempt to divert the course of the hearings did not, however, erase from the minds of the committee members the issue Ellender had raised before McGovern's intervention. As soon as McGovern's question was answered, Senator Young asked Freeman and then Bell to assess the extent of the foreign aid character of the program. Both insisted that the program served not only foreign but domestic interests as well and, therefore, refused to estimate the proportions of the program relating to foreign and domestic interests. Hence, Senator Ellender decided to probe deeper into the problem:

> In connection with what Senator Young has stated to Mr. Bell about the use of these funds, we have a lot of funds in Egypt. I was disappointed when I found out, when I was in Egypt, that we have quite a few ships going through the Suez Canal. We have a lot of Egyptian money on hand—that is, Egyptian pounds—and yet we cannot use those pounds to pay for the cost of our ships going through the Suez Canal. It would seem to me that these funds would be used for any purpose we desired in these countries.[21]

Director Bell, admitting unfamiliarity with this problem, made no attempt to refute Ellender's criticism and, therefore, offered to look into the matter of surplus currency use in Egypt. The questioning of Bell and Freeman was concluded when Senator Aiken asked about the possibility of expanded use for Title I currencies. Again, the answers of the two representatives of the Executive agencies were polite and imprecise.

Basically, there were two items that bothered Chairman Ellender during the Senate hearings: (1) dissatisfaction with the role of the Department of State, and (2) the so-called inefficiency and unbusinesslike manner which he saw in the Food for Peace operations.

The attitude of the spokesmen for the Administration, on the other hand, reflected recognition of the power of the Senate committee and resignation to their inability to sway the committee members to accept the Administration's image of the program.

Perhaps because of the limited time scheduled for the hearings, perhaps because the outcome was predetermined, fewer interest groups testified before the Senate committee than did before the House. Of the eleven interest groups giving actual testimony before the committee, only three represented farm organizations—the remainder were voluntary agencies. Eight additional groups, however, submitted statements to be inserted into the record; of these, five represented farm groups and the remainder, voluntary agencies.

While the general positions of these groups remained much the same as those in the House, a few differences should be pointed out. While most of the voluntary agencies expressed support in the House for the period of extension requested by the Executive, there was relatively little reference to this item in testimony before the Senate; the groups merely urged the extension of the program. It is interesting to note, however, that the National Farmers Union—the only farm group supporting the Executive request before the House committee— did not testify via a personal representative; it merely filed a written statement containing remarks similar to the testimony before the House. The Grange continued its relatively mild opposition to certain aspects of the program, and the Farm Bureau maintained its position of opposition to the program. Of the new groups testifying, the President of the International Economic Policy Association, Dr. N. R. Danielian, commented that he thought: "A program of such magnitude should have the benefit of Congressional scrutiny more frequently than every five years."[22] Finally, several maritime groups appeared to oppose the provision of the Senate bill eliminating the financing of a portion of the ocean freight charges by the United States government.

Modifications forthcoming

As has been pointed out, the tone of the Senate committee hearings indicated that serious modifications in the original Senate bill would be forthcoming.[23] Of the ten Executive proposals contained in the Senate bill as introduced, only three were retained unchanged by the committee: the removal of the limitation on Cooley loans, authorization of the use of Title I currencies for internal security purposes, and authorization to expand the payment of general average contributions. The provisions permitting sale of Title I currencies to voluntary agencies and to United States flag vessels were deleted. The Senate committee removed the specification that the annual reports contain details on the exchange rates for Title I, replacing it, however, with a more restrictive provision which subjected all Title I currencies to the appropriations process. The Senate committee also changed the provision for the period of extension of Titles I and II from five to two years—a reduction of one year from the then-existing program. Furthermore, the Senate committee added three new provisions to the bill: (1) a stipulation that the United States obtain the highest legal exchange rates on Title I negotiations possible and a rate not less than that obtained by any other government; (2) a stipulation to prohibit the restrictions as to the use of the United States portion of Title I currencies; and (3) a stipulation requiring Public Law 480 to be classified in the President's budget as expenditures for international affairs and finance rather than agriculture.

Thus it would seem that while the House committee bill represented a victory for the Administration, the Senate bill constituted the first major defeat for the Executive agencies. The greatest irony, perhaps, lies in the manner in which the Senate committee reacted to the Executive request. In Senator Ellender's original bill, all ten items requested by the Executive agencies were incorporated only *pro forma*. After the setback inflicted by the Senate committee, all hope for strengthening the Executive position in the Senate was, for all practical purposes, eliminated because of the powerful position of Senate committees in the legislative process.

THE FLOOR OF THE HOUSE OF REPRESENTATIVES

As suggested above, the Administration was relatively happy with the legislation on the 1964 extension of Public Law 480 reported out of the House Committee on Agriculture. In contrast to the Senate committee bill, the House committee bill represented a document the Administration hoped would be enacted into law. However, when H.R. 12298 was debated on the floor, practically all optimism vanished.

There were two attempts to pass the House bill on the floor. The first occurred on August 17 when Representative Cooley made a motion to suspend the rules and pass H.R. 12298. Since under suspension of the rules no amendments can be added on the floor, this was no doubt a strategic move on the part of the supporters of the Administration to avoid restrictive modification of H.R. 12298. Thus, during the first forty minutes of heated debate, strong criticisms were directed toward the committee bill in an effort to spoil passage under suspension of the rules and bring the bill to the floor under a procedure permitting revision.

Three such criticisms emerged: (1) the failure of the House bill to stipulate Congressional appropriations control over the use of Title I currencies; (2) the allegation that the law was used as a foreign aid program rather than for the purpose of disposing of surplus United States agricultural commodities; and (3) the criticism that the program provided assistance to nations hostile or indifferent to the goals of the United States. The first two of these criticisms were linked together in a major attack led by Representative Frank T. Bow (R-Ohio) who served on the Appropriations Committee. Bow referred to the bill as a complete back-door spending program because the expenditures authorized under the three-year program did not go through the Appropriations Committee item by item. Bow and others also criticized the provision of the House bill establishing an advisory committee as a measure to limit the freedom of Congress to pass upon the use of Title I currencies. This general line of criticism was amplified by the allegation that the absence of such provisions was predicated upon the desire to use the program for foreign aid, which supposedly was to the detriment of United States agricultural interests.

As customary, the House committee bill was defended by the author of the bill—in this case, Chairman Poage.

> I believe that the Appropriations Committee has a good deal to do in this House. It has pretty nearly all that the members can handle in the time that they have, and sometimes they do not get it done. They are way behind right now with most of the work. . . . In other words, they are so far behind right now that they have to talk about continuing resolutions next month, not this month, yet they want more authority.[24]

The third line of criticism was led by Paul Findley in the same style and tone as the one incorporated in his minority report. His chief argument was against Public Law 480 aid to nations hostile to the United States or which were either communist or communist-leaning.

These criticisms had their intended effect when the forty minutes expired and the vote was taken. Of the 153 congressmen present, eighty-two voted to adopt the bill under suspension of the rules, while seventy-one voted against the measure; thus, the maneuver to circumvent the amendment of the committee bill on the floor fell twenty votes short of the 102 votes required for the two-thirds majority.

Amendments and debate

The second attempt to pass H.R. 12298 took place September 2 and 3. The bill was passed September 3 after two days of confusing floor action, during which several restrictive amendments were added. Four major issues emerged. The most controversial debate on the floor of the House was an attempt led by Representative Findley to insert into the House bill a provision identical to that of the Senate bill which would have subjected all Title I currencies to the appropriations process. In submitting his proposal on September 2, Findley stated that, "It would do away with much of the back-door spending of this program so far as it dealt with the disposition of U.S.-owned foreign currencies."[25] As formulated, the Findley amendment would have eliminated the provision of the House committee bill establishing a Presidential Advisory Committee. Findley's amendment was strongly supported by Representatives Rooney (D-New York), Bow and Whitten (D-Mississippi)—all using the argument of back-door spending.[26] Congressmen opposing the Findley amendment were Cooley, Poage, Albert (D-Oklahoma), Matthews, and Jones of Missouri. These members expressed concern over the effects such a provision would have on the operations of the program and defended the committee provision for the Advisory Committee as entirely adequate for the supervision of currency uses. The opponents of the Findley amendment further argued that acceptance of such a proposal would have the result of increasing the accumulations of Title I currencies and reduce the number of Title I agreements, thereby aggravating the United States surplus problem. The Findley amendment was accepted by a teller vote of 125 yeas and ninety-six nays.

On September 3, however, the House reversed itself with respect to this provision. Strangely enough, the move to eliminate the Findley provision was led by Representative John J. Rooney who introduced a substitute bill with the following remarks:

> This pending substitute for Section 1 substantially contains the bill as it has been approved up to this point . . . , with one exception, and that is the exclusion of the so-called Findley amendment adopted yesterday.

I must be frank and say that I supported the Findley amendment yesterday. Today, I find that I cannot support it for the reason that on South Vietnam 90 percent of the local currency funds generated under Title I sales, Public Law 480, is used to support the military effort there.[27]

By eliminating the Findley amendment which was a replacement for the provision establishing an Advisory Committee, however, the Rooney proposal effectively eliminated both provisions. Representatives Mahon (D-Texas and Chairman of the Appropriations Committee), Cooley, and Poage expressed their support for the Rooney substitute. No congressman spoke on behalf of Findley, except Findley himself. The Rooney substitute was accepted by voice vote.

A second issue on the floor of the House was aid to Poland and Yugoslavia. This issue was introduced by Congressman Findley in the form of an amendment prohibiting Title I and IV sales to communist countries. Unlike in the subcommittee hearings on the House floor, Findley was unrestricted in presenting his case. The debate on this issue was brief, since Findley and Cooley were the only two congressmen expressing views on the matter. Findley's proposed amendment was rejected by a voice vote. Findley, however, refused to yield. After the House bill was ordered to be engrossed and read for the third time, Findley moved to recommit the bill with instructions to insert the provisions of his amendment. He also demanded a roll-call vote. There was no debate. In the subsequent vote, 183 congressmen voted to accept the Findley provision, 175 voted against it, one answered "present," and seventy-one did not vote.[28] The provision restricting Title I and IV sales to Poland and Yugoslavia was therefore incorporated into the final House bill.

Assistance restricted

A third major issue on the floor of the House was the restriction of Public Law 480 assistance to "aggressor nations." This was aimed at the United Arab Republic (UAR) because of actions which had been inimical to foreign-policy interests of the United States. This issue entered the legislative process in the form of an amendment proposed by Oliver P. Bolton (R-Ohio), stating explicitly that Public Law 480 aid could not be extended to the UAR. The thrust of Bolton's argument, which was supported only by Representative Farbstein (D-New York), was that by providing aid to Egypt the United States freed funds which Nasser used for aggression against nations friendly to the

United States, i.e., Israel, Yemen, and Saudi Arabia. Representatives Cooley, Gallagher (D-New Jersey), Multer (D-New York), Matthews and Joelson (D-New Jersey), and Adair (R-Indiana) rose in opposition to the Bolton amendment arguing against the exclusion of a country by specific name.

On September 3, Representative Roosevelt (D-California) offered a substitute to the Bolton amendment which had the effect of eliminating Public Law 480 aid to all nations unless the President determined they were not (1) aggressors (in a military sense) against any country having diplomatic relations with the United States, or (2) using funds of any sort from the United States for purposes inimical to the foreign policy of the United States. This substitute amendment, therefore, would have eliminated the UAR from Title I programs without specific reference to the country. The Roosevelt substitute was supported by Representatives Pucinski (D-Illinois), Joelson, and Gallagher. Representatives Rosenthal (D-New York) and Gross (R-Iowa) opposed the Roosevelt substitute as not strong enough. Those congressmen, unequivocally opposed as they were to this provision, made no comments on the Roosevelt substitute, apparently because they realized opposition at this stage was futile. Thus the substitute was accepted by a voice vote.

The fourth major issue on the floor of the House was whether to remove the existing 25 percent limitation on the use of Cooley funds. On September 2, Representative Whitten submitted an amendment which, in effect, would have reinstated the 25 percent limit removed by the House bill, with an additional stipulation that Title I currencies could not be used to promote or increase production of agricultural commodities if the recipient nation was exporting such commodities in competition with the United States. Congressman Whitten supported his amendment with an extensive excerpt from a report he was preparing for the House Appropriations Committee. This report documented the manner in which Cooley loans had restricted American private enterprise in numerous countries. Representative Cooley was the only congressman rising in opposition to the Whitten amendment. He argued that provisions in the existing law restricted such use of Cooley loan funds and, therefore, there was no reason to oppose removal of the limitation. In spite of Cooley's efforts, the House accepted the Whitten amendment by a voice vote.

In addition to the four major issues, three other amendments were considered by the House of Representatives. Representative Rogers (D-Mississippi) submitted an amendment on September 2 which proposed to prohibit Public Law 480 sales to any nation permitting its ships or aircraft to visit Castro's Cuba. This amendment was accepted by a voice vote. On the same day, Representative Findley proposed an amendment which would have adopted the provisions of the Senate bill regarding the period of extension and authorization of funds for Titles I and II. This amendment was defeated by a voice vote. Finally, on September 3, Congressman Derwinski (R-Illinois) proposed to sell accumulations of foreign currencies in communist countries to individuals who owned and operated farms in these countries. Derwinski's amendment was rejected by a voice vote.

On September 3, the House passed H.R. 12298, tabled it, and moved to consideration of the Senate bill which had been passed on August 19. The House then amended the Senate bill by striking out everything but the enacting clause and inserted the entire House bill as passed.

THE FLOOR OF THE SENATE

The Congressional response as expressed on the floor of the Senate, on August 19, was quite different from that of the House of Representatives. Whereas, on the floor of the House the chief concern was over the leniency of the committee bill, in the Senate the concern was over the restrictions imposed by the committee bill. Debate in the Senate revolved around three issues: (1) whether to subject all Title I currencies to the appropriations process, (2) Title I and IV interest rates, and (3) ocean freight charges.

The issue concerning the appropriations process was debated more than any other issue. George McGovern was the only senator to express direct opposition to the provisions of the Senate bill subjecting all Title I currency grants to the appropriations process. His comments reflected the feelings of a past Director of the Food for Peace program.

What this new, unprecedented provision in the bill does is to provide, in effect, for a double appropriations process. It not only does that, but it also hamstrings the administrators of the program who have been doing an increasingly effective job. It ties the hands of the President in using these grants in a flexible and imaginative way to encourage economic development, to promote the mutual defense programs in which our country is cooperating with other countries. In every way it represented the introduction of more red tape, more of the kind of delay to which the senator from Minnesota was referring, it means more procrastination, less efficiency and less effectiveness for the total program.[29]

Senators Humphrey and Fulbright (D-Arkansas) were more indirect in their opposition to the appropriations provision. Their tactics were to support the committee provision of the House bill which provided for a Presidential Advisory Committee. Humphrey and Fulbright conveyed the hope that the House provision would be adopted in conference. No defense of the appropriations provision was made on the floor of the Senate. Apparently the supporters of the provision relied on the strength of the justification contained in the committee report:

> The purpose of this amendment [to the bill as introduced] is to provide the same degree of control over grants of U.S.-owned foreign currencies as is provided in the regular foreign assistance legislation over dollar grants; also to coordinate all foreign assistance grants and to assure that grants of foreign currencies are being used in place of dollar grants rather than being supplementary thereto. Further, the making of such grants subject to Congressional appropriation control will not only require that such grants be justified before a Congressional committee but will also have the effect of reimbursing the Department of Agriculture in part for the cost of the commodities, the sale of which generated the currencies in question.[30]

The second major issue discussed on the floor of the Senate dealt with the provision specifying minimum interest rates with respect to Title I and IV loans. Senator McGovern and Senator Humphrey were the only two spokesmen in opposition to the provisions of the committee bill specifying that Title I and IV loans bear a rate of interest no lower ". . . than interest paid by the United States government on money it borrowed."[31] Senator Humphrey spoke first:

> We have gone through the battle on foreign aid many times. If we are to insist upon an interest rate on Title I loans and Title IV credits to be the interest rate that is paid by the U.S. government on the money it borrows, we shall be making loans which will not be repaid.[32]

Senator McGovern endorsed Humphrey's criticism of the committee bill. He added that such a provision would be detrimental to United States agriculture and foreign policy as well.

A third issue raised on the floor of the Senate was the provision prohibiting the CCC from financing ocean freight charges on Title I shipments, except to cover the portion of such costs in excess of freight rates charged by foreign vessels—the excess attributable to the use of higher-rate American vessels under the Cargo Preference Act. Senators McGovern, Warren G. Magnuson (D-Washington), E. L. (Bob) Bartlett (D-Alaska), and George Aiken (R-Vermont) expressed the fear that such a provision would remove a necessary subsidy for the American merchant marine and would further handicap American shippers by requiring them to negotiate with recipient countries for payment in hard currencies.[33]

The opponents of these three Senate bill provisions, however, made no attempt to amend them out of the bill on the floor, probably because they felt it would be useless. Two minor amendments, however, were proposed and accepted on the floor of the Senate: The first one, proposed by Senator Aiken, made a minor change in the language of the provision of the Executive request to remove the 25-percent limitation on Cooley loans. The second one, sponsored by Senator Jacob K. Javits (R-New York), stipulated that Public Law 480 be used for the purpose of making friendly nations independent of trade not only with the USSR, but also with Communist China.

Once the Senate had passed S. 2687 by a voice vote, the bill was sent to conference. Insertion by the conference committee of the House provision, excluding Poland and Yugoslavia from Title I sales and sharply curtailing Title IV sales to them, sparked a debate on the Senate floor unprecedented in the history of Food for Peace deliberations. The attack against this provision was led by Senator Fulbright when the conference bill was considered by the Senate on September 23 and 24. After a lengthy examination of the conference report, coupled with some strong remarks, Fulbright reprimanded his colleagues for lack of wisdom in the conduct of foreign affairs:

> It is an outrageous procedure to come into the Senate with such a report and with so little opportunity for the Executive branch, which is responsible for these relations, to be heard. Those in charge of the program are condemned daily in the press for being inefficient. Now the Congress comes along and in this proposed out-of-hand fashion, without any real consideration of what is involved, attempts to impose this kind of obstruction on the conduct of our foreign relations.[34]

Fulbright then proposed that the Senate refuse to pass the conference bill until it had been referred to the Committee on Foreign Relations and hearings had been held on the matter. The senators expressing agreement with the Fulbright recommittal were Clark (D-Pennsylvania), Cooper (R-Kentucky), Monroney (D-Oklahoma), McGovern and Hart (D-Michigan), and Keating (R-New York). Senator Aiken expressed sympathy for Fulbright's position but opposed the recommittal because he feared it would prevent acceptance of the bill before adjournment. Senators Johnston, Hickenlooper and Morse expressed their support for the conference bill. Yet, the Senate, by a roll-call vote (24 yeas, 46 nays and 30 abstentions), rejected the recommittal motion. Fulbright, therefore, asked the Senate to reject the conference report in the hope that the conference committee could be induced to change its mind. Again, by a roll-call vote, the Senate rejected Fulbright's proposal and accepted the conference bill, 54 to 11 with 35 not voting.

THE CONFERENCE COMMITTEE

While the two chambers of Congress were still debating H.R. 12298 and S. 2687 on their respective floors, it became apparent that there were going to be major differences between the two bills. Thus, when the House passed its bill and amended it into the Senate bill, the Speaker of the House appointed the following conferees: Cooley, Poage, Matthews, Hoeven, and Dague (R-Pennsylvania). Since the Senate failed to accept the House version of the bill, it requested, by a voice vote, a conference with the House. Consequently, on September 10, the Presiding Officer appointed Senators Ellender, Johnston, Holland, Eastland, Talmadge, Aiken, Young of North Dakota, and Hickenlooper as conferees for the Senate.

The conduct of business in the conference committee was governed by elaborate rules which limit the alternatives open to conferees. One such limitation, for example, was the voting procedure requiring majority agreement among the conferees of each House (called managers) on each issue. Another limitation imposed by the rules was that only dissimilar items in the two bills could be the subject of conference action. Once agreement was reached by the conference committee, then the compromise bill was returned to both Houses in the form of a conference report. A further restriction prohibited the amendment of the conference bill on the floor of either House. If there was dissatisfaction with the report, it could only be rejected *in toto* and referred back to conference for further action by the managers.

Seven issues of difference

The House and Senate bills, as passed, differed on seven important issues. These issues were resolved by the conference committee.[35] These "conference issues" included the following: (1) the period of extension of Titles I and II; (2) the restriction of aid to communist nations; (3) Congressional control of Title I currency grants; (4) the rate of interest on Title I and IV loans; (5) the restriction on granting Public Law 480 assistance to aggressor nations; (6) removal of the 25-percent limitation on Cooley loans; and (7) budget classification of Public Law 480 expenditures.[36] Since there were no minutes of debate kept in the conference committee, an analysis of conferee debates cannot be presented. An attempt will be made in the following chapter, however, to analyze the role of individual managers from their responses to questionnaires.

The first issue resulted in the adoption by the conference committee of a provision, originally proposed in the Senate bill, for Title I extension and authorization which specified a $2.7 billion plus carryover expenditure commitment for a two-year period. The House bill would have authorized $4 billion plus carryover for a three-year period, while the Executive had requested $7.5 billion plus carryover for a five-year period.

The period of extension for Title II was also set at two years, with an authorized commitment of $400 million annually. Whereas the period of extension came from the Senate bill, the amount of Title II authorization was a compromise between the House and the Senate provisions. The Executive request for Title II was $450 million annually for each of five years. Thus it was apparent that the conference chose to adopt the more restrictive of the two alternatives.

The second issue produced a conference report provision for the exclusion of both Poland and Yugoslavia from Title I sales. With respect to Title IV sales, Yugoslavia was permitted to continue in normal transactions, and Poland, which was ineligible for Title IV sales under other laws, was given the option to participate in Title IV sales with a five-year credit limitation. The conference committee thus modified the Findley floor amendment to the House bill which would have excluded Poland and Yugoslavia from both Title I and IV sales. Furthermore, the conference document prohibited Title I sales to any nation allowing its ships or aircraft to visit Cuba, so long as it was controlled by the Castro regime. This provision also modified a House floor amendment which had been proposed by Representative Rogers by excluding Title IV sales from the prohibition. Executive opposition to such provisions had been voiced by Undersecretary Harriman in the House hearings.

The third issue—that of Congressional control of Title I currency grants—was resolved by the managers of the House and Senate by the creation of a Presidential Advisory Committee. This committee was to be composed of the Secretary of Agriculture, the Administrator of AID, the Director of the Bureau of the Budget, and the Chairman and ranking minority member of the House and Senate Agriculture Committees. The duties of this committee, as spelled out by the conference bill, authorized the study of excess currency problems; no powers of Presidential recommendation, however, were granted to this committee. The President was required to consult with this committee on matters relating to economic development and private industry loans of Title I currency, on convertibility of Title I currencies, and with respect to interest rates on Title I and IV loans. Another provision of the conference report, pertaining to Title I currencies, required that Congress be given the opportunity to disapprove within a specified limit of time all Title I agreements before they were signed by recipient countries.

These two conference provisions cleared up one of the most complex Congressional issues debated during the entire legislative process. All three major participants had taken different positions on this issue. Representatives of the Executive agencies had strongly opposed any restriction on Title I currency grants during the course of the hearings. The Senate bill would have subjected all Title I currency grants to the appropriations process. In the case of the House, the defeat of Representative Findley's effort to incorporate the Senate provision into the House bill on the floor eliminated a provision for a Presidential Advisory Committee. By providing for the Advisory Committee, however, the conferees revived a provision of the House bill which had been deleted on the floor. Nevertheless, the conferees' failure to provide the Advisory Committee with power to make recommendations to the President (on grants and other uses of excess currencies) modified the original House provision into a less restrictive method of controlling Title I currency grants.

The fourth issue resolved by the conference committee related to the interest rates on Title I and IV loans. The House and Senate managers adopted the Senate provisions specifying that such interest rates must not be lower than that paid by the United States government on the money it borrowed. However, provision was made for the acceptance of a lower rate, if such rate was recommended by the Advisory Committee. During the course of the hearings, Administration officials expressed opposition to both of these provisions.

Revision inserted

As a result of the fifth issue, the conferees inserted into their revision of the House and Senate bills a provision which prohibited Public Law 480 sales (but not other programs) to nations which the President determined to be waging military aggression against nations friendly to the United States or which were using funds obtained from the United States in a manner inimical to the foreign policy interests of the United States. This provision was merely an affirmation of existing procedure which permitted Presidential option on whether or not to make such determination. The conference report, therefore, substantially modified a provision accepted on the floor of the House which would have required the President to make such a determination in order to prevent the halting of *all* Public Law 480 programs in any given country. As has been pointed out, this provision was aimed primarily at the United Arab Republic.

The sixth issue stemmed from the elimination on the floor of the House of a provision—contained in the original Executive request— to remove the 25-percent limitation on Cooley loans. The conferees reinserted this provision and deleted the House amendment which provided that no Cooley funds could be used to develop in recipient countries agricultural production which was competitive with United States commercial exports. This provision of the conference report corresponded with that in the Senate bill.

The seventh and final major issue resolved by the conference related to the budget classification of Public Law 480 expenditures. The conference report contained the Senate provision requiring all Public Law 480 expenditures to be classified in the President's budget under international affairs and finance (foreign aid) rather than under agriculture. (This was already the case with Title II foreign donation programs.) This measure was indirectly opposed by the Executive in the course of the hearings.

There were five additional items incorporated into the conference report: (1) the prohibition of United States financing of ocean freight charges, except to the extent that costs for transportation on United States vessels exceeded the rates of other nations; (2) a requirement that Title I agreements negotiated with the UAR would make provision for the use of resultant currencies in payment of United States costs for use of the Suez Canal; (3) the inclusion of Communist China among the nations from which Public Law 480 recipients were to be freed in trade relations; (4) a provision permitting Title III assistance to be used for self-help projects designed to eliminate the need for foreign aid in recipient countries; and (5) the authorization of $7.5 million per year of CCC funds under Title II to purchase Title I currencies for the support of more effective use of food made available under Titles II and III. The first three of these items came from the Senate bill and the last two from the House bill.

Another six items were included in both the House and Senate bills as passed and were therefore automatically incorporated into the conference report. Three of these were also contained in the Executive request: (1) the provision to permit use of Title I currencies to be used in support of internal security programs; (2) the authorization of payment of general average contributions for Title III programs; and (3) provision of an annual rather than semiannual Presidential report on activities carried out under Public Law 480. The other three items, which were of no great consequence, were: (1) a stipulation that Title I exchange rates must not be less than the legal rate obtained by other countries; (2) a provision that 20 rather than 10 percent of the Title I currencies within any country must be reserved for United States use and subject to the appropriations process; and (3) a provision for the sale of Title I currency to United States tourists.

All issues resolved by the conference committee can be summarized under one heading: *increased Congressional control and supervision of Public Law 480 operations*. This restriction of the program was admitted by the managers on the part of the House in their report to the whole House:

> The general effect of the conference substitute herewith reported is to substantially expand Congressional control over supervision and operation of Public Law 480 and to take numerous steps to assure that the United States receives the maximum possible benefits from the surplus commodities exported under this act.[37]

On September 23, the conference report was returned to the House of Representatives. In contrast to the Senate, reaction to the conference report in the House was almost perfunctory. Yet, there was at least one event that deserves special mention. On the same day, Congressman Findley was congratulated by third- and seventh-ranking members of the Republican hierarchy in the House for the superb job he had performed on behalf of the minority party. Representative Hoeven uttered the following words:

> In this connection I want to take this opportunity to commend the gentleman from Illinois (Mr. Findley) on the outstanding work he did in getting his amendment (on aid to communist nations) inserted in the bill when it was considered in the House. The gentleman from Illinois (Mr. Findley) has rendered a great public service in bringing this important matter to the attention of Congress and the American people.[38]

Congressman Halleck (R-Indiana), in addition to praising Findley for the success of his effort to bar Public Law 480 aid to the communist nations, commended the influence Findley exerted on the adoption of the two-year extension and the creation of the Advisory Committee.[39] After considering other routine matters, the House adopted the conference report by a voice vote.

The presentation of the conference report in the Senate stimulated lively debate. In addition to Senator Fulbright's effort to obtain reconsideration of the conference bill, there were other dissatisfactions on the part of other senators with the conference bill. The comment of Senator McGovern is a typical example:

> What [the Executive needs] is a strong Congressional mandate to move ahead even more decisively and imaginatively in using our God-given food abundance as a tool for peace and humanity and as a justified reward for the efficiency of the American farmer.
>
> If we restrict and hamstring and weaken Food for Peace, we are hurting the American farmer, jeopardizing the U.S. taxpayer, hurting our friends abroad, and undercutting international interests.
>
> Yet, this latter course is the one we have taken in this year's Congressional assault on Food for Peace.
>
> The Food for Peace conference report now before us is a great disappointment.[40]

Nevertheless, on September 24, the Senate, by a roll-call vote (54 to 11), accepted the conference report and sent it to the President.

SUMMARY AND CONCLUSIONS

During the 1964 extension and amendment of Public Law 480 by Congress in response to the Executive request, the major arguments waged in the legislative process were centered around two types of issues: (1) those generated by the ten items submitted in the Executive request, and (2) those derived from the examination of the program itself.

What did the Executive receive from the Congress? Was the Congress sympathetic to the Administration's request? Or, did the Congress use this opportunity to reveal its disenchantment with the program? What were the things about Public Law 480 that bothered the Congress most? Was the Congress united or divided on the major issues? What norms governed the Congressional response to the Executive request? What were the tone and atmosphere within which arguments were exchanged?

As Table 5.1 reveals, only two items (numbers 18 and 19 of the Executive request) were approved by the Congress without any changes. Two other requests (numbers 21 and 16) were recommended by the Congress in their original form after changes had been eliminated. Two of the Executive proposals (numbers 24 and 25) were completely deleted from the conference bill and four items (numbers 1 through 4) were modified by the Congress. Obviously, Congress was not overly anxious to please the Administration and thus, in the final analysis, it decided to impose restrictions upon the Administrative discretion in Public Law 480 programs. These restrictions were contained in the fifteen new provisions which the Congress added to the document submitted to the President for ratification. It is, therefore, reasonable to assume that there was Congressional concern about certain aspects of the Public Law 480 program. This becomes evident from a close scrutiny of the Congressional debates. The concentration of time, effort and energy devoted to deliberations, as well as the tone of the dialogues, reveals a distinction among issues resolved during the legislative process.

Seven issues out of twenty-eight were highly controversial. One of the seven—the period of extension for Titles I and II—was generated by Executive request. The remaining six issues were derived from Congressional scrutiny. One of these six—the rates of interest on Title I and IV loans—was a borderline issue since it involved relatively little Congressional controversy in spite of Executive protest to Congressional decision. Another issue—budget classification of Public Law 480 expenditures—is relatively unimportant in terms of Congressional controversy, although it touches upon the central problem of the 1964 extension and amendment. Thus the five most controversial issues in the Congressional response were: (1) Congressional control of Title I currency grants; (2) aid to communist countries; (3) the period of

TABLE 5.1

The Executive request as compared to the conference bill in terms of provisions

Executive Request	Conference Bill
1. Requested a five-year extension of Title I (through December 31, 1969)	1. Provides a two-year extension for Title I (through December 31, 1966)
2. Requested a five-year extension of Title II (through December 31, 1969)	2. Provides a two-year extension for Title II (through December 31, 1966)
3. Requested for Title I an authorization of $7.1 billion for a five-year period with a limit of $2.5 billion for any one year, plus carryover of unused funds from prior years	3. Provides an authorization for Title I of $2.7 billion for a two-year period with a limit of $2.5 billion for any one year, plus carryover of unused funds from previous years
4. Requested for Title II an authorization of $450 million for each of five years	4. Provides for Title II an authorization of $400 million for each of two years
5. No provision	5. Prohibits sales under Title I to any communist country or any country which permits its ships or aircraft to travel to Castro's Cuba, but provides that such countries shall be eligible for Title IV sales (other laws notwithstanding)
6. No provision	6. Prohibits sales under Title I or Title IV to any country determined by the President to be an aggressor against any country having diplomatic relations with the U.S. or using funds obtained from the U.S. for purposes inimical to U.S. foreign policy
7. No provision	7. Limits financing of ocean freight charges on certain Food for Peace shipments to the differential by which the U.S.-Flag rate exceeds the rates of ships from other countries
8. No provision	8. Requires exchange rates for Title I sales to be the highest legally obtainable and not less favorable than those which any other country obtains

TABLE 5.1 (*continued*)

Executive Request	Conference Bill
9. No provision	9. Establishes an Executive-Legislative advisory committee to assist the President in reducing excess Title I currencies; this committee must be consulted by the President with respect to policies on economic development, interest rates on loans, degree of convertibility of currencies, etc.
10. No provision	10. Provides that proposed uses of Title I currencies for grants (except military grants) or proposed use of loan repayments for any purpose must be submitted to the House and Senate committees on agriculture with either committee having the right to disapprove
11. No provision	11. Increases from 10 to 20 percent the minimum amount of Title I currencies subject to the appropriations process
12. No provision	12. Requires that Title I currencies be convertible to the extent consistent with the purposes of the act, and in any event to such an extent as is necessary to meet obligations or charges payable by U.S. government agencies in recipient countries
13. No provision	13. Requires that Title IV loans bear a rate of interest not less than the minimum rate required for development loans under the Foreign Assistance Act
14. No provision	14. Requires Title I currency loans to bear a rate of interest not less than the cost of funds to the U.S.
15. No provision	15. Authorizes the use of $7.5 million per year of CCC funds to be used for the purchase of Title I currencies to be used in support of Title II and III programs

TABLE 5.1　*(continued)*

Executive Request	Conference Bill
16. Requested that the 25-percent limitation on Cooley loans be removed	16. Removes the 25-percent limitation on the amount of funds which may be used for Cooley loans
17. No provision	17. Authorizes the sale of Title I currencies to U.S. tourists
18. Asked that use of Title I currencies in support of counterinsurgency programs be authorized	18. Authorized the use of Title I currencies in support of counterinsurgency program
19. Requested that authority to pay general average contributions be extended to Title III	19. Provided that general average contributions payments could be extended to Title III
20. No provision	20. Provides that Title I shall be used to assist friendly nations to be independent of trade with Communist China as well as the USSR
21. Asked that the Presidential reports be made annual rather than semiannual	21. Specifies that Presidential reports shall be annual rather than semiannual
22. No provision	22. Permits Title III commodities to be used for self-help projects designed to alleviate the need for food aid
23. No provision	23. Requires expenditures under PL 480 to be classified in the President's budget under international affairs and finance rather than under agriculture
24. Requested that sale of Title I currencies to voluntary agencies be authorized	24. No provision
25. Requested that sale of Title I currencies to U.S.-Flag vessels be authorized	25. No provision

SOURCE: For the provisions of the conference bill, see *Annual Report, op. cit.,* pp. 96-7. For the provisions of the Executive request, *cf. Senate Hearings, 1964, op. cit.,* pp. 5-6.

extension for Titles I and II; (4) the restriction of Public Law 480 aid to aggressor nations; and (5) the removal of the 25-percent limitation on Cooley loans.

Dilemma revealed

All five issues seem to point in one direction. They reveal the continuing dilemma of how much of the Public Law 480 plan is domestic and how much is foreign policy. Congress never met this problem head on. The only decision made by Congress which came close to this problem was the requirement that the President in his budget charge Public Law 480 operations to foreign aid rather than agriculture. Realizing that Public Law 480 was not exclusively an agriculture program and served foreign relations as well as domestic agriculture, Congress has justified continuation of the program year after year under the pretense that it was a "good" program serving both interests. Thus the facade of surplus disposal was as useful to the Congress as it was to the Executive. Another possible explanation for Congressional hesitancy to make this an issue was the risk involved in gambling away Agriculture Committee jurisdiction of Public Law 480. Hence, frustrated by the trend of Public Law 480 operations toward the use of the program as an instrument of foreign policy, Congress used these five issues to increase its own control.

The manner in which these issues were resolved represents certain norms of Congressional behavior. In the House of Representatives, for example, many procedural inconsistencies could be observed. Such inconsistencies pointed to the importance of the five issues. Contrary to general practice, none of the representatives of the minority party (who were appointed to the subcommittee because of their specialized knowledge) played a major role either in the hearings or on the floor of the House. Instead, two members of the Agriculture Committee were the leaders of the Republican opposition to the Administration. These were Representative Hoeven, who as ranking minority member of the full committee had every reason to attend the hearings, and Congressman Findley whose presence can be attributed to a combination of voluntarism and excess enthusiasm in a freshman congressman. Both Congressman Hoeven and Findley were responsible for significant modifications of the program. Their actions in the subcommittee hearings can be interpreted as part of an overall partisan strategy. To impose such strategy on the subcommittee, where minimal partisanship is normally in evidence, was another violation of

House tradition. This violation, however, was not strong enough for any committee disapproval of Hoeven's actions to emerge in the records of the hearings. It is not evident that either Hoeven or Findley informed Chairman Poage of his intention to carry his disagreements to the floor. Such behavior is not conducive to subcommittee unity.

On the floor of the House, additional unorthodox practices were noteworthy. For example, two of the five major issues were introduced for the first time on the floor in spite of the established custom to air major issues first in committee. The House reversed itself on two major issues; in one instance passing and then rejecting an amendment and, in the other, rejecting and then passing a provision. Such *volte-face* is not common on the floor of the House of Representatives.

More agreement in Senate

In the House also, there were serious deviations from the rules of conduct, probably because of the existing vast differences of opinion and dissatisfaction with the committee bill on the part of the remainder of the House. On the other hand, in the Senate, violation of the rules was less common because most senators found themselves in agreement with the committee bill and also because of the committee's strategic role in the legislative process. The Senate as a whole followed and approved the recommendations of the Committee on Agriculture and Forestry primarily because, in the absence of a subcommittee on Public Law 480, the committee was the sole source of authoritative advice on Public Law 480. Therefore, key Senate decisions on the major issues concerning the extension and amendment of Public Law 480, for all practical purposes, were made in Senator Ellender's committee. His power as committee chairman was aptly demonstrated in three stages of the Senate handling of the extension of Public Law 480. Senator Ellender wrote the Senate version of the bill, dominated the hearings, and was instrumental in the management of the bill on the floor.

In view of Ellender's enormous power as committee chairman, it is fair to conclude that his decision to incorporate all ten items of the Executive request into his bill for the sake of expediency was a departure from regular Senate procedure. The only peculiar behavior on the floor was Senator Fulbright's effort to have the conference report recommitted for consideration by the Committee on Foreign Relations. As was pointed out by his colleagues, the acceptance of this proposal would have set a new precedent in the Senate.

Turning to the Congress as a whole, no serious infractions of accepted norms and procedures can be discerned. Although there were numerous deviations from standard legislative procedures in both the House and the Senate, these contradictions failed to affect intracongressional relationships. On the contrary, the precedent of unifying behind the decision of the majority was exemplified in this instance.

The departure from established rules and procedures in the House and the Senate is paralleled by the tone of arguments waged among the proponents and opponents to the Executive request. It would appear that as an issue increases in significance, not only will Congressional norms and mores be violated, but the tone of argumentation will become more indignant. Two cases support this hypothesis. In the House subcommittee hearings, for example, the discussion deteriorated into a name-calling contest when Findley attempted to introduce the issue of aid to communist nations.

> MR. FINDLEY: You [Freeman] stated in that speech, according to this report that I have been selected as the hatchetman to twist and distort figures to help the Republican Party. . . . Where did I admit being the hatchetman of the Republican Party?
> SECRETARY FREEMAN: I never said that you admitted it. . . .
> MR. POAGE: . . . unless your discussion is relevant, I do not see why you should come to this hearing and ask to get it in the record. You cannot come here as a cuckoo and lay your eggs in this basket.
> MR. FINDLEY: I have been called the hatchetman, and now a cuckoo bird, so it would be quite a challenge for an artist to paint my picture. . . .
> MR. POAGE: While I want to say that you are welcome, you are not a member of this subcommittee. You have not, as a member of subcommittee, been maligned in any way. . . . I am sure that you went to church the day before yesterday, and you did not raise the question there in that meeting. I think your discussion would have been about as much in order there as it is here.
> We will be glad to hear from you, Mr. Jones.[41]

The second case occurred on the floor of the Senate during Senator Fulbright's attempt to recommit the conference bill. In response to a plea from Senator Mansfield to reconsider his motion, the Chairman of the Senate Foreign Relations Committee retorted:

> MR. FULBRIGHT: Mr. President, I insist upon my motion that the conference report be referred to the Committee on Foreign Relations for hearings and study.

I shall not sit idly by and have a foolish thing done in this manner and have the Committee on Agriculture and Forestry impose upon one of the most important aspects of our foreign relations. I think this is unacceptable procedure.

If there is not a quorum present, the Senate can adjourn. We have been doing it for two weeks. It would not be anything unusual.[42]

The above two cases, however, are not typical of the entire Congressional response. They represent an exception rather than the rule. Nevertheless, they are important because these two, as well as other occasional examples of impolite tone in the Congressional debates, assist us in evaluating the seriousness of the controversial issues.

Although the above analysis of the Congressional response leads to certain conclusions, caution is required so as not to apply these conclusions as general rules of Congressional behavior. There are many other factors and variables which influence the legislative process. If one recalls, for example, that 1964 was a Presidential election year, that the Republicans were the minority party, that several Public Law 480 recipients expressed sympathy for communism, and others were preparing for aggression, one will recognize that the explanations provided here for certain Congressional behavior are inconclusive. Thus, analysis in depth of the voting behavior in legislative decision-making units is a prerequisite for a more definitive explanation of the Congressional response.

Chapter 6

The Congressional Response: Voting Behavior

SINCE VOTING was the major tool for resolving issues in all five decisional units of Congress, the analysis of voting behavior on the 1964 extension and amendment of Public Law 480 is imperative. Among the many types of voting procedures employed by the Congress, the following were used to extend and amend Public Law 480 in 1964: voice, teller, division, and roll call. Since only the latter provides voting results of individuals, roll-call analysis is the most desirable method for describing and measuring variations in the voting behavior of individual congressmen, groups of congressmen, and variations among roll calls. But there were only four roll calls and no two were strictly comparable. Therefore, a roll-call analysis of the Public Law 480 extension in 1964 is, for all practical purposes, impossible. Hence, the analysis essentially will be derived from responses to a mail questionnaire and intensive open-end interviews.[1]

ISSUE POSITIONS OF DECISIONAL UNITS IN THE CONGRESS: SURVEY ANALYSIS

During the hearings on the 1964 extension of Public Law 480 held by the House Subcommittee on Foreign Agricultural Operations, there were three issues debated in response to the Executive request. These were:

1. Whether or not to continue Public Law 480 assistance to the communist nations of Poland and Yugoslavia.

2. Whether or not to establish an executive-legislative advisory committee for the supervision and control of Title I currency utilization.

3. Whether the period of extension and financial authorization for Titles I and II should be the same as requested by the Executive.

The common issue around which these three were centered was:

111

4. Whether Public Law 480 was essentially a domestic or foreign program.

As Table 6.1 reveals, the opinions of the subcommittee members were divided most sharply on the extension period requested by the Administration (issue #3). Of the three Democrats on the sub-committee who responded to the questionnaire, two favored reduction of the Executive request. One of the three responding Republicans, however, supported the Administration on this issue. One liberal Democrat and one conservative Republican supported the Executive request, and two conservative Republicans and two conservative Democrats opposed it.[2]

On issue #2, two Democrats and one Republican expressed their support for the establishment of an executive-legislative advisory committee. Only one Democrat opposed this measure and two Republicans expressed no opinion. Insofar as a "no" reflects a liberal position, there was only one liberal congressman supporting the Administration's interest. Two conservative Democrats and one conservative Republican were in favor of establishing an executive-legislative advisory committee. Two conservative Republicans expressed no opinion on this issue.

On the issue of Public Law 480 aid to communist nations (issue #1), all but one of the Democrats expressed support for continuation of such aid while all three Republicans opposed it.[3] Assuming that conservatives desired to discontinue aid to Poland and Yugoslavia, there were only three out of five conservatives who conformed to this expectation. All three were Republicans. Both conservative congressmen who supported aid to communist nations were Democrats. There was only one liberal Democrat who expressed opposition to the continuation of such aid.

Issue #4 reflects a fairly decisive stand on the part of the sub-committee members since only one out of six, a conservative Republican, identified the program as both domestic and foreign. The only congressman who perceived the program as essentially domestic was a conservative Democrat.

In the Senate Committee on Agriculture and Forestry, two new issues were introduced:

5. Whether or not to subject grants of foreign currencies to Congressional approval via the appropriations process. This issue is closely related to issue #2 (the establishment of an executive-legislative advisory committee). Both were treated in Chapter 5 under the general heading of Congressional control of Title I currencies.

TABLE 6.1

Issue Position of the House Subcommittee on Foreign Agricultural Operations

		1			2			3		4		
Issues	Yes	?	No	Yes	?	No	Yes	?	No	Domestic	Both	Foreign
Democrats	2	0	1	2	0	1	1	0	2	1	0	2
Republicans	0	0	3	1	2	0	1	0	2	0	1	2
Total	2	0	4	3	2	1	2	0	4	1	1	4
Liberals	0	0	1	0	0	1	1	0	0	0	0	1
Conservatives	2	0	3	3	2	0	1	0	4	1	1	3

Respondents*

* Out of ten members of the House subcommittee nine answered the inquiry, however, only six responded to the questionnaire. Congressmen Frank A. Stubblefield (D-Kentucky) and Ralph R. Harding (D-Idaho) failed to answer—Representatives Page Belcher (R-Oklahoma) and Paul C. Jones (D-Missouri) answered but did not respond to the questionnaire.

SOURCE: The conservative-liberal categorization is based on data contained in the *Congressional Quarterly Almanac*, vol. xx, 1964, pp. 755-61.

6. Whether or not to continue Public Law 480 aid to nations either waging aggression against nations having diplomatic relations with the United States, or nations using United States funds of any type for purposes inimical to United States foreign policy.

As illustrated in Table 6.2, the most decisive division in the Senate committee was on issue #3. There were seven Democrats favoring the requested extension period of Public Law 480, and two were opposed. None of the Republicans opposed it; however, one Republican expressed no position. Unlike members of the House subcommittee, most of the conservatives favored the Administration request.[4] Four conservative Democrats and one conservative Republican favored the five-year extension; whereas, two conservative Democrats were opposed and one conservative Republican was undecided. All three liberal Democrats were for the five-year extension. Despite the strong support for the Executive request as mentioned in Chapter 5, the Senate committee bill extended Public Law 480 for only two years.

On issue #5, six conservative Democrats and one conservative Republican supported the Congressional supervision of Title I currency grants by means of the appropriations process. All three liberal Democrats and one conservative Republican opposed this measure. Since a "no" response meant support of the Administration, all liberals responded according to expectations.

With respect to the cessation of aid to aggressor nations (issue #6), five conservative Democrats and two conservative Republicans responded favorably, and all three liberal Democrats, as well as one conservative Democrat, were in opposition.

There were four conservative Democrats who favored, three liberal Democrats who opposed, and two conservative Democrats who also opposed the establishment of an executive-legislative advisory committee (issue #2). One conservative Republican responded in favor of the issue, and one was undecided. As noted in Chapter 5, the Senate committee rejected this proposal in favor of issue #5 when the bill was reported out of committee.

Unlike that in the House subcommittee, the perception of issue #4 in the Senate committee was undecisive and blurred. Three conservative Democrats, one liberal Democrat, and one conservative Republican viewed the Public Law 480 program as both domestic and foreign. Four Democrats, two liberal and two conservative, regarded the program as primarily domestic; and one conservative Democrat and one conservative Republican felt the program was basically foreign.

TABLE 6.2

Issue Positions of the Senate Committee on Agriculture and Forestry

Issues	2			3			4			5			6		
	Yes	?	No	Yes	?	No	Domes-tic	Both	For-eign	Yes	?	No	Yes	?	No
Democrats	4	2	3	7	0	2	4	4	1	6	0	3	5	0	4
Republicans	1	1	0	1	1	0	0	1	1	1	0	1	2	0	0
Total	5	3	3	8	1	2	4	5	2	7	0	4	7	0	4
Liberals	0	0	3	3	0	0	2	1	0	0	0	3	0	0	3
Conservatives	5	3	0	5	1	2	2	4	2	7	0	1	7	0	1

Respondents*

* Out of seventeen members of the Senate committee twelve answered the inquiry. However, only eleven responded to the questionnaire. Senators Caleb J. Boggs (R-Delaware), James O. Eastland (D-Mississippi), J. Howard Edmondson (D-Oklahoma), Bourke B. Hickenlooper (R-Iowa), and Milton R. Young (R-North Dakota) failed to answer. Senator George D. Aiken (R-Vermont) answered, but did not respond to the questionnaire.

SOURCE: The conservative-liberal categorization is based on data contained in the *Congressional Quarterly Almanac*, vol. xx, 1964, pp. 755-61.

In the conference committee, two new issues were added to the Congressional response. They were:

7. Whether or not to remove the 25-percent limitation on Cooley loans.

8. Whether or not to prohibit the use of foreign currencies for the production of commodities in recipient countries if such commodities were competitive with United States commodities.

Both of these issues were discussed in Chapter 5 under the general heading of Cooley loans.

Among the nine respondents of the conference committee, there were four senators and five congressmen. Since a majority of the managers of both Houses was required on any compromise before legislation could be returned to the floor in the form of a conference report, and since all respondents of the conference committee were conservatives,[5] only party and House-Senate divisions are of significance.

As Table 6.3 shows, the most clear-cut issue in the conference committee was #7. On this issue, seven Democrats and one Republican favored the removal of the 25-percent limitation on Cooley loans. Only one Republican opposed the measure. All four senators approved, as did all but one congressman.

On issue #6, both Republicans and five Democrats opposed continuation of aid to aggressor nations, and two Democrats favored the continuation of such aid. Whereas, one senator and one congressman were opposed, three senators and four congressmen favored the measure.

Congressional control of Title I currencies through the appropriations process (issue #5) was approved by five Democrats and both Republicans. Two Democrats responded against the measure. All four senators supported the provision as did three congressmen. The two leading Democratic congressmen, however, disapproved of this provision.

All but three of the Democratic conferees agreed that the period of extension (issue #3), requested by the Executive, should be reduced. Both Republicans were opposed to the Administration on this issue. Only one congressman and two senators favored the five-year extension period.

On the question of continuing aid to communist nations (issue #1), the Democrats split three to four, and both Republicans joined the opposition.[6] All of the senators were opposed. Three congressmen favored continuation of such aid and two were opposed.

TABLE 6.3

Issue Positions of the Conference Committee

Respondents* Issues	1 Yes	1 ?	1 No	2 Yes	2 ?	2 No	3 Yes	3 ?	3 No	4 Domestic	4 Both	4 Foreign
Democrats	3	0	4	5	1	1	3	0	4	2	3	2
Republicans	0	0	2	1	1	0	0	0	2	1	0	1
Totals	3	0	6	6	2	1	3	0	6	3	3	3
Senators	0	0	4	3	1	0	2	0	2	1	2	1
Congressmen	3	0	2	3	1	1	1	0	4	2	1	2

Respondents* Issues	5 Yes	5 ?	5 No	6 Yes	6 ?	6 No	7 Yes	7 ?	7 No	8 Yes	8 ?	8 No
Democrats	5	0	2	5	0	2	7	0	0	2	0	5
Republicans	2	0	0	2	0	0	1	0	1	2	0	0
Totals	7	0	2	7	0	2	8	0	1	4	0	5
Senators	4	0	0	3	0	1	4	0	0	2	0	2
Congressmen	3	0	2	4	0	1	4	0	1	2	0	3

* Out of thirteen members of the conference committee, ten answered the inquiry. However, only nine responded to the questionnaire. Senators Eastland, Hickenlooper, and Young failed to answer. Senator Aiken answered but did not respond to the questionnaire.

Five Democrats favored, one was undecided and one was opposed to the establishment of the executive-legislative advisory committee (issue #2). One Republican was undecided, and the other approved of the measure. Three senators and three congressmen supported the advisory committee, and one of each expressed no opinion. Only one congressman was opposed.

Five of the seven Democrats disapproved of the measure to prohibit the use of United States-owned foreign currencies for the production of commodities in recipient countries if such commodities were competitive with United States-produced commodities (issue #8). Both Republicans supported the prohibition. Two senators were in favor and two were opposed. Three representatives expressed a negative opinion and two a positive one.

With respect to issue #4, two Democrats felt Public Law 480 was primarily a domestic program; two viewed it as a foreign aid program; and three felt it was both. One Republican identified the program as domestic and the other one as foreign aid. One senator and two congressmen labeled the program as domestic, and one senator and two congressmen called it foreign aid. Two senators and one representative, however, identified the program as both.

ISSUE POSITIONS OF DECISIONAL UNITS IN THE CONGRESS: ROLL-CALL ANALYSIS

There was a total of four roll-call votes taken in the Congress on matters relating to the 1964 extension of Public Law 480.[7] Two of these were in the Senate and two in the House. While two roll-calls (one in the House and one in the Senate) dealt with issue #1—whether or not to continue aid to communist nations—the other two roll-calls were votes on the House and the conference version of the final bill.

On the floor of the House, 175 congressmen expressed their support for the continuation of Public Law 480 aid to Poland and Yugoslavia; however, 183 were opposed. Of the 175, 13 were Republicans and 162 were Democrats. Of the latter, 108 were Northern Democrats and 54 were Southern Democrats. The opposition to the continuation of such aid consisted of 143 Republicans and 40 Democrats. Only six of the latter were Northern Democrats. There were 72 representatives who failed to vote: 52 Democrats and 20 Republicans.

On the floor of the Senate, 26 Democrats and 20 Republicans voted against the continuation of Public Law 480 aid to Poland and Yugoslavia. There were 15 Northern Democrats and 11 Southern Democrats joining the Republican opposition. Only five Republicans, five Southern Democrats, and fourteen Northern Democrats supported the existing policy. Of the 30 senators who did not vote, 21 were Democrats and 9 Republicans.

The final version of the House bill was accepted by a margin of 343 votes.[8] There were two Southern Democrats who joined four Republicans in opposition. Among the 75 congressmen who did not vote, 54 were Democrats and 21 were Republicans.

The Senate accepted the conference bill by an overwhelming majority of 54 to 11.[9] All 24 voting Republicans supported the bill. There were 16 Northern Democrats and 14 Southern Democrats in favor of the bill and 9 Northern Democrats and 2 Southern Democrats voting in opposition to the bill. Among the nonvoting senators, 25 were Democrats and 10 Republicans.

PATTERNS OF CONGRESSIONAL SUPPORT AND OPPOSITION IN THREE DECISIONAL UNITS

Conclusions derived from the foregoing analysis must be interpreted with 70 percent accuracy. Although 80 percent of all members of the three decisional units (the House subcommittee, the Senate committee, and the conference committee) in the Congress answered the inquiry, only 70 percent of them responded to the questionnaire.

On the basis of the questionnaire responses, there emerge certain patterns of Congressional behavior which are predicated upon support, indifference, and opposition to the Executive desire to expand the foreign aid aspect of the program. These patterns are based on an index score reflecting a frequency count of responses from each legislator to every issue incorporated in the questionnaire.[10] An index score is equivalent to the prevailing number of responses to all issues in any category after cross-cancellation of responses.

In the House subcommittee, the following pattern becomes apparent. On the one hand, congressmen supporting the Administration were: Matsunaga (+4) and Poage (+2). On the other, representatives opposing the Administration were: Dague (−6) and McIntire (−4). Congressmen whose overall position was neither for nor against the Executive included: Harvey (±2) and Matthews (±0).

In the Senate committee, the Executive-support pattern was as follows: McCarthy (+6), McGovern (+6), Neuberger (+6), and Cooper (+2). The pattern of Executive opposition included: Ellender (−4), Walters (−4), Holland (−2), and Talmadge (−2). In between were: Johnston (±0), Jordan (±0), and Mechem (±0).

The House conferees lineup was as follows. In support of the Administration were: Poage (+2) and Cooley (+2). In opposition were: Dague (—6) and Hoeven (—6). Matthews (±0) was in the middle of the road. The Senate conferees in opposition were: Ellender (—4), Holland (—2), and Talmadge (—2). Johnston (±0) was in the middle.

Although these index scores are not completely in harmony with the index scores of Presidential support and opposition (as constructed by the *Congressional Quarterly Almanac*) there is significant correlation between the two. The same holds true with respect to conservative coalition scores also from the *Almanac*.

Another discrepancy

Another discrepancy exists between some committee decisions and the distribution of questionnaire responses. In the Senate committee, for example, on issue #3 eight respondents supported the five-year extension, while only two opposed it; yet the committee bill was reported out with a two-year extension provision. It is conceivable, therefore, that the influence of Chairman Ellender and Senator Holland was determinant in this case. Similarly, in the conference committee on issue #5, the influential position of Chairman Cooley and Poage, as the sole opponents of the Congressional supervision of currencies by means of the appropriations process, may have been instrumental in deleting this provision from the conference bill altogether.

As Table 6.4 reveals, the intensity of the controversy of issues was as follows: numbers 2 and 5, 3, 1, 6, 7, and 8. The underlying issue with the greatest controversial intensity was #4.

Numerous factors and variables were important in shaping these patterns of Congressional response.[11] Among these, ten were hypothesized as being more germane than others.

As Table 6.5 reveals, *chi* square (X^2) was used as the tool to determine whether a statistically significant relationship existed between the issue positions of 11 Senate committee respondents and 10 variables which were hypothesized to have had a causal influence on the decision makers of this group. Only four variables qualified for the generally accepted 5-percent (.05) level of probability as the standard of significance. This means that the distribution of the dependent variables (in the rows), when measured against the independent variables (in the columns), results in a X^2 that is significant at the 5-percent level of probability when $p < .05$ is presented in this way. We may assume, therefore, that the relationship specified between the variables

TABLE 6.4

Issue positions of key decision makers in Congress on Public Law 480

Issues	1			2			3			4		
	Yes	?	No	Yes	?	No	Yes	?	No	Domestic	Both	Foreign
Respondents*	7	0	12	10	4	5	10	0	8	5	7	7

Issues	5			6			7			8		
	Yes	?	No	Yes	?	No	Yes	?	No	Yes	?	No
Respondents*	10	0	8	13	0	6	17	1	1	8	0	11

* Out of 29 (17 senators and 12 congressmen) 19 responded (11 senators and 8 congressmen).

is real rather than chance, or that the chances are at least 100 to 5 the result of the respondents' issue position rather than of the chances of sampling. The four most significant variables in the Senate Agriculture Committee were: liberal-conservative (p < .001), Presidential sup-

TABLE 6.5

Relationship of ten variables to Senate Agriculture Committee issue positions

	Issues No.	Executive support	Indifference	Executive opposition	χ^2	d/f	P
	Issue 2.	3	3	5			
	Issue 3.	8	1	2			
Relationship	Issue 4.	2	5	4			
	Issue 5.	4	0	7			
	Issue 6.	4	0	7			
	Total	21	9	25			
	1. ND	12	1	2			
Party	2. SD	6	5	19	17.22	4	.001 < .01
	3. R	3	3	4			
Party unity	4. Yes	21	9	25	0.00	2	—
	5. No	0	0	0			
Liberal- conservative	6. Liberal	12	1	2	15.31	2	< .001
	7. Conservative	9	8	23			
Presidential support	8. Support	18	1	11	16.20	2	< .001
	9. Opposition	3	8	14			
Attendance at hearings	10. Present	19	9	22	1.16	2	.30 < .50
	11. Not Present	2	0	3			
Occupation	12. Farm	5	2	8	.52	2	.70 < .80
	13. Non-farm	16	7	17			
Farm constituency	14. Farm	15	6	14	1.22	2	.50 < .70
	15. Non-farm	6	3	11			
P.L. 480 constituency	16. Non-farm	6	3	11			
	17. Top ½ P.L. 480	4	1	0	5.41	4	.20 < .30
	18. Bottom ½ P.L. 480	11	5	14			
Age	19. −50 yrs. old	8	0	1			
	20. 50-70 yrs. old	10	8	12	17.85	4	.001 < .01
	21. +70 yrs. old	3	1	12			
Seniority	22. −6 yrs.	13	4	8			
	23. 6-12 yrs.	5	3	7	5.33	4	.20 < .30
	24. +12 yrs.	3	2	10			

Source: The ten variables are based on data contained in *Congressional Quarterly Almanac,* vol. xx, 1964; and Appendices VI and VII.

port (p < .001), political party (.001 < p < .01), and age (.001 < p < .01). Whereas Public Law 480 constituency and seniority have some relationship to the respondents' issue position (.20 < p < .30), occupation and farm constituency, for all practical purposes, had no relationship significance.

In the House Subcommittee on Foreign Agricultural Operations (Table 6.6), none of the 10 variables had a significant relationship to the distribution of issue preferences. The relationships closest to the statistical level of significance were exhibited by two variables: Presi-

TABLE 6.6

Relationship of ten variables to the House Agricultural Subcommittee issue positions

	Issues No.	Executive port support	Indifference	Executive opposition	χ^2	d/f	P
Relationship	Issue 1.	2	0	4			
	Issue 2.	1	2	3			
	Issue 3.	2	0	4			
	Issue 4.	1	1	4			
	Total	6	3	15			
Party	1. ND	2	0	2			
	2. SD	3	0	5	5.97	4	.20 < .30
	3. R	1	3	8			
Party unity	4. Yes	6	3	15	0.00	2	—
	5. No	0	0	0			
Liberal-conservative	6. Liberal	2	0	2	1.92	2	.30 < .50
	7. Conservative	4	3	13			
Presidential support	8. Support	5	0	7	5.73	2	.05 < .10
	9. Opposition	1	3	8			
Attendance at hearings	10. All days	5	0	7	5.73	2	.05 < .10
	11. Some days	1	3	8			
Occupation	12. Farm	1	2	5	2.25	2	.30 < .50
	13. Non-farm	5	1	10			
Farm constituency	14. Farm	2	2	4	1.80	2	.30 < .50
	15. Non-farm	4	1	11			
P.L. 480 constituency	16. Non-farm	4	1	11			
	17. Top ½ P.L. 480	1	0	3	6.60	4	.10 < .20
	18. Bottom ½ P.L. 480	1	2	1			
Age	19. −50 yrs. old	2	0	2			
	20. 50-70 yrs. old	4	3	13	1.92	4	.70 < .80
	21. +70 yrs. old	0	0	0			
Seniority	22. −6 yrs.	3	2	3			
	23. 6-12 yrs.	2	0	2	6.23	4	.10 < .20
	24. +12 yrs.	1	1	10			

SOURCE: The ten variables are based on indices contained in *Congressional Quarterly Almanac*, vol. xx, 1964; and Appendices VI and VII.

dential support and attendance at hearings ($.05 < p < .10$). Public Law 480 constituency and seniority had the next highest relationships ($.10 < p < .20$). The variables of political party, liberal-conservative, and farm constituency had a low correlation to the subcommittee issue positions.

Tests of significance of variable relationships in the conference

TABLE 6.7

Relationship of ten variables to conference committee issue positions

| | Issues No. | Senate | | | χ^2 | d/f | P |
		Executive support	Indifference	Executive opposition			
Relationship	Issue 1.	0	0	4			
	Issue 2.	0	1	3			
	Issue 3.	2	0	2			
	Issue 4.	1	2	1			
	Issue 5.	0	0	4			
	Issue 6.	1	0	3			
	Issue 7.	0	0	4			
	Issue 8.	2	0	2			
	Total	6	3	23			
Party	1. ND	0	0	0			
	2. SD	6	3	23	0.00	4	—
	3. R	0	0	0			
Party unity	4. Yes	6	3	23	0.00	2	—
	5. No	0	0	0			
Liberal-conservative	6. Liberal	0	0	0	0.00	2	—
	7. Conservative	6	3	23			
Presidential support	8. Support	3	0	5	3.13	2	.20 < .30
	9. Opposition	3	3	18			
Occupation	12. Farm	2	1	13	1.39	2	.50 < .70
	13. Non-farm	4	2	10			
Farm constituency	14. Farm	2	3	11	3.71	2	.10 < .20
	15. Non-farm	4	0	12			
P.L. 480 constituency	16. Non-farm	4	0	12			
	17. Top ½ P.L. 480	0	0	0	3.71	4	.30 < .50
	18. Bottom ½ P.L. 480	2	3	11			
Age	19. −50 yrs. old	0	0	0			
	20. 50-70 yrs. old	2	3	11	3.71	4	.30 < .50
	21. +70 yrs. old	4	0	12			
Seniority	22. −6 yrs.	0	0	0			
	23. 6-12 yrs.	1	1	6	.35	4	.98 < .99
	24. +12 yrs.	5	2	17			

committee (Table 6.7) were conducted in two separate groups: the Senate and House conferees. Such procedure was necessitated by the decision-making process in Congress. While there was no significant correlation between variables and issue positions of Senate conferees, there were two variables with statistically significant relationships in the House conference group. Presidential support (.001 < p < .01) and political party (.02 < p < .05) were strongly related to Executive support, indifference and opposition. There was a relatively weaker correlation between Public Law 480 constituency and House conferee

TABLE 6.7 (*continued*)

	Issues No.	House Executive support	Indifference	Executive opposition	χ^2	d/f	P
	Issue 1.	3	0	2			
	Issue 2.	1	1	3			
	Issue 3.	1	0	4			
	Issue 4.	2	1	2			
Relationship	Issue 5.	2	0	3			
	Issue 6.	1	0	4			
	Issue 7.	4	0	1			
	Issue 8.	3	0	2			
	Total	17	2	21			
	1. ND	0	0	0			
Party	2. SD	15	1	8	9.93	4	.02 < .05
	3. R	2	1	13			
Party unity	4. Yes	17	2	21	0.00	2	—
	5. No	0	0	0			
Liberal-conservative	6. Liberal	0	0	0	0.00	2	—
	7. Conservative	17	2	21			
Presidential support	8. Support	15	1	8	9.93	2	.001 < .01
	9. Opposition	2	1	13			
Occupation	12. Farm	0	0	0	0.00	2	—
	13. Non-farm	17	2	21			
Farm constituency	14. Farm	13	1	10	0.00	2	—
	15. Non-farm	14	1	11			
	16. Non-farm	14	1	11			
P.L. 480 constituency	17. Top ½ P.L. 480	7	0	1	5.43	4	.20 < .30
	18. Bottom ½ P.L. 480	6	1	9			
	19. —50 yrs. old	0	0	0			
Age	20. 50-70 yrs. old	17	2	22	0.00	4	—
	21. +70 yrs. old	0	0	0			
	22. —6 yrs.	0	0	0			
Seniority	23. 6-12 yrs.	3	0	5	.75	4	.90 < .95
	24. +12 yrs.	14	2	16			

SOURCE: The ten variables are based on indices contained in *Congressional Quarterly Almanac,* vol. xx, 1964; and Appendices VI and VII.

issue positions. The strongest correlation in the Senate conference group was between the group's issue positions and the farm constituency variable ($.10 < p < .20$).

SUMMARY

This chapter sought to answer questions relating to the patterns of voting during Congressional response. What was the intensity of influence of factors and variables on the Congressional issue positions? In particular, were Congressional decision makers more affected by party division than liberal-conservative variables; more by farm constituency than by nonfarm constituency; more by Presidential support than by age; more by seniority than by occupation?

Although the raw data sheet revealed certain patterns of Congressional behavior in the four groups of Congressional decision makers, there was no way of assessing from the data sheet the measure of influence our hypothesized variables exerted on the decision makers. Hence, the simplest method of correlation—"*chi*-square distribution" of statistically significant relationships between respondents' issue positions and selected variables—was used to answer the above questions. In spite of the great rigor and accuracy of statistical expression of voting behavior in Congress, the *chi*-square method, in this instance, as in all others, did not measure facts but the representation of data used for testing hypotheses. Thus, any conclusions derived by this method must be interpreted as indicators only, rather than valid generalizations. Nevertheless, these indicators can be useful as evidence for a new theory.

It would seem from Tables 6.5 through 6.7 that the variables may be ranked in intensity of influence in the following order: Presidential support, attendance at hearings,[12] political party and Public Law 480 constituency, age, farm constituency, liberal-conservative and seniority, occupation and, finally, party unity.

Verbal analysis not borne out

Although the verbal analysis of the Congressional debates indicated stronger overall liberal-conservative correlation than political party relationship, this was not borne out by the *chi*-square analysis of the respondents' issue positions. The influence of political party variable was almost twice as strong as that of liberal-conservative influence on the Executive support and opposition in the three Congressional committees. This was the case in spite of the paradoxical position of the Southern Democrats who were even more strongly opposed to the Administration than were the Republicans. This explains the extremely low correlations obtained for the variable of party unity.

It was hypothesized, from the firm support for domestic aspects of Public Law 480 programs during Congressional debates, that there would be a strong correlation between the distribution of issue positions and the agricultural constituency interests of the decision makers.

This hypothesis was only partially validated. While the variable of Public Law 480 constituency and political party exhibited about the same degree of correlation as did political party, the farm versus non-farm constituency variable was of very low significance. The comments of one able Congressional aide shed some light on this contradiction: "Many congressmen are critical of the program but continue to vote for it."[13] In addition, it should be pointed out that Congress has, for several years, used surplus disposal as a facade for the foreign aid aspects of the program. However, Congress did not go as far as to permit a fundamental change in the program and thus curtailed the Executive attempt to make Public Law 480 primarily an instrument of foreign policy.

Assuming that the 1964 Executive request for Public Law 480 legislation was not atypical, it was hypothesized that Presidential support scores would be highly correlated with issue positions. The *chi*-square analysis confirmed this hypothesis with the highest score of influence. It was further assumed that the older members of the Congress would have the stronger tendency to oppose changes in an existing program. The analysis indicated that this hypothesis had some validity—it ranked in the middle. Surprisingly, however, seniority, which was expected to play a similar role, manifested a considerably lower degree of correlation.

What conclusions can be reached from the preceding analyses? It would seem from the patterns of support and opposition to the Executive request that the Senate committee (21-9-25) was more in favor of the Administration's proposals than was the House subcommittee (6-3-15). The reverse, however, was the case with respect to the bills actually reported out by the two committees. To explain this apparent contradiction, one must take into account the powerful positions of the chairmen of the Senate committee and the House subcommittee. Since Chairman Poage ranked second in Executive support among subcommittee members, it can be assumed that he exercised his influence upon his colleagues to the advantage of the Administration. However, the opposite can be argued for Senator Ellender who was the highest ranking opponent of the Executive request. Hence, the Senate committee bill was less generous than that of the House subcommittee.

Chapter 7

Executive Prospects for Future Legislative Support

CHAGRIN, RESENTMENT, AND PROTEST characterized the reaction of the Administration to the Congressional decision on the 1964 extension and amendment of Public Law 480. Two provisions in particular were criticized by the Chief Executive as "unconstitutional" and, therefore, to be legitimately ignored by the Administration. One provision required that both proposed grants of foreign currencies acquired under Title I and uses of loan repayments be subject to veto by the agriculture committees of the House and the Senate. The other provision prohibited the President from making Title I loans at an interest rate below a specified level, unless a lower rate was approved by an executive-legislative advisory committee. Furthermore, President Johnson expressed his disappointment with the provision prohibiting the sale of United States farm commodities for foreign currencies under Title I to any communist nation. He felt that this restriction would inhibit "... our ability to deal selectively with countries that may demonstrate a tendency toward political and economic independence from communism."[1] In spite of these reservations, however, the President had no practical alternative but to sign the bill into law. It is thus evident that the Congressional decision did not conform to the Executive desire. Before attempting to extrapolate the prospects for Public Law 480 from the 1964 extension and amendment—the task of this final chapter—let us review the Congressional attitude toward the program during its ten-year history.

. Examination of CCC holdings of surplus agricultural commodities, seems to indicate that the magnitude of surplus stocks has remained relatively constant for the period from 1956 to 1964. During this same period, however, Public Law 480 annual authorizations for Title I programs continued to increase although at a lower rate from 1962 on. Hence, it would be inaccurate to link the size of Public Law 480 causally only to the size of surplus agricultural holdings. The Congressional and Executive attitudes toward the magnitude of Public Law 480 were affected by other factors and variables than the United States domestic agricultural considerations.

Foreign policy instrument

Since 1957, surplus agricultural commodities have played an increasingly important role as an instrument of United States foreign policy toward the developing nations of the world. As soon as United States foreign economic aid policy picked up momentum, Public Law 480 annual authorizations for Title I programs began to increase. It is thus reasonable to assume that such programs have become more and more an instrument of United States foreign policy and less and less a tool for concessional sales of domestic agricultural products.

Around 1956, the shift in United States foreign policy objectives—from military assistance and containment of communism in Europe, to economic aid and assistance in developing nations—came as a result of new world tensions created by unequitable relationships between the "have" and "have not" nations. The disproportionate increase of population, as compared to food production, in many diet-deficient regions of the world, has been one of the keys to tensions affecting the United States in the arena of world politics. To cope with this problem effectively, the United States developed the Food for Peace program in 1961, primarily as an adjunct to its foreign policy apparatus.

The total Food for Peace and Public Law 480 commitments from July 1, 1954 through December 31, 1964 amounted to $17,137.8 million. Although the foreign aid aspect of Public Law 480 was always high (approximately 85 percent of the annual total), it was relatively higher (89.9 percent) during the period of Food for Peace. This increase in the use of Public Law 480 as an instrument of foreign policy has taken place under the auspices of a law originally passed for somewhat different purposes.[2] While the continued relationship of food aid to surplus disposal (under one program) has gained support from congressmen generally opposed to foreign aid, it has also aggravated certain inherent conflicts between domestic and foreign interests and has postponed resolution of fundamental issues. A survey of the Congressional attitudes, prior to 1964, reveals six chronic points of tension between the "old guard," who saw the program as essentially a surplus disposal device for alleviating the problems of United States agriculture, and the "young turks," who wanted to expand the foreign aspect of the program as an instrument of United States foreign policy.

Recurrent in the four extensions of Public Law 480, prior to 1964, were the questions of whether: (1) to have short or long-term extensions; (2) to provide assistance to communist nations; (3) to expand the role of Congress in supervising program operations; (4) to curb programs producing accumulations of foreign currencies; and (5) to instigate organizational changes for greater efficiency in program operations. Directly or indirectly, all these questions had bearing on whether the program should be utilized more for concessional sale of surpluses as part of domestic agricultural policy, or for the donation of surplus food as a tool of foreign policy. Such issues remained unresolved because of the lack of acuteness, coupled with unwillingness on the part of all concerned to risk the losses which might result from resolution.

Did the 1964 extension and amendment resolve these chronic issues? If so, how were they resolved? If not, why not? Were any new issues introduced in 1964? If so, were they resolved?

EXECUTIVE-LEGISLATIVE INTERACTION IN 1964

All but one of the five chronic issues were considered during the 1964 extension and amendment. The Congress did not consider instigating major organizational changes in the program in 1964. While the 1964 legislation contained provisions affecting the remaining four issues, one cannot conclude that such provisions constituted the final resolution. In 1964, once again the central issue—whether to expand or cut back the foreign aid aspects of the program—was sidestepped. In 1964, neither opponents nor proponents of the foreign aid aspect of the program chose to force the issue, probably because both felt insecure about the outcome of a direct confrontation. Instead, both factions restrained their argumentation to a merely probing level of intensity in the effort to keep the lid on Pandora's box. Consequently, several new issues emerged during the debates. Three were more controversial than the others: (1) aid to aggressor nations; (2) the rates of interest on Title I and IV loans; and (3) the removal of the 25 percent limitation on Cooley loans. Of these three, only the issue dealing with the limitation on Cooley loans was resolved in such manner as to preclude recurrence.

Congressional hesitancy to confront the fundamental issues of the program buttressed the position of the congressmen desiring to reduce its foreign aid aspects. The probing techniques employed by both the opponents and proponents of the use of Public Law 480 as an instrument of foreign aid had the effect of curtailing the Executive request through all stages of the legislative process. In addition, the position of the proponents was handicapped by the Administration's decision not to use an aggressive strategy in the hearings. A possible explanation for this behavior on the part of the Executive lies in the centrifugal forces operating within the administrative structure of Food for Peace. Paradoxically, therefore, it would appear that the Executive was forced by circumstance to contribute to the reduction in 1964 of the expansion of the foreign aid aspects of the program.

What were the factors and variables which determined the 1964 Congressional response? One of the main factors contributing to the final legislative product was the influence exerted by the chairmen of the committees. Senator Ellender, as chairman of the Senate Committee on Agriculture and Forestry, played a major role in the modification of the Executive request. His opposition to the Administration provided a rallying point for both Republicans and Southern Democrats on the committee who together overwhelmingly outnumbered the Northern Democrats. In the House committee and subcommittee, on the other hand, Chairmen Cooley and Poage neither endorsed nor completely opposed the Executive request. Both were critical of certain aspects of Public Law 480 operations; however, when the die was cast, both defended the Administration position. While this situation produced a committee bill favorable to the Administration, such a reserved endorsement opened the floodgates for the adoption of restrictive measures on the floor of the House.

Other factors and variables which were equally important in determining the outcome of the 1964 extension and amendment included: (1) Presidential support; (2) political party; (3) Public Law 480 constituency; and (4) the age of committee members. The analysis in Chapter 6 showed the balance of power in the committees held by the Southern Democrats. Thus the attitude of the Southern Democrats to Public Law 480 is important —providing the key to the 1964 Congressional response.

The respective roles played by the Southern Democrats in the House and in the Senate were antithetical. On the one hand, in the House subcommittee, the Southern Democrats who responded to the questionnaire sided more often with the Northern Democrats than they did with the Republicans; they generally supported the Presidential position on legislation; they came from Public Law 480 constituencies; and they were middle-aged. In the Senate, on the other hand, the Southern Democrats sided with the Republicans more often than with the Northern Democrats; with the exception of one, they opposed the Presidential legislative position; all but two came from

Public Law 480 constituencies; all of them were conservatives; and all but one around the age of 70. Thus it came as no surprise that the Senate committee bill was more unfavorable than the House committee bill to the Executive.

Three affecting factors

Since 1964, the Food for Peace program has been affected by three major changes. First, the magnitude of United States government holdings of surplus food has declined to a "normal" level. This change led to speculation that if the Food for Peace program was to continue, nonsurplus commodities might have to be purchased by the government on the open market, thus making the program an adjunct to regular foreign aid. On the other hand, it was suggested that this decline, when coupled with continued food deficits in many foreign countries, could lead to planned surpluses through an expansion of agricultural production in the United States. In preparation for coping with this problem, Executive Order No. 11252 on October 20, 1965, was initiated, transferring the functions of the director of the Food for Peace program (Richard W. Reuter) to the State Department. One of his major tasks was to develop a ". . . philosophy and policy of United States food aid as a component of United States foreign policy."[3]

On February 10, 1966, a third change affecting the future of the program was introduced in a message to Congress from President Johnson. This message requested the Congress to enact in 1966 a new Food for Freedom program to replace Public Law 480. While based on the Public Law 480 legislation, the Food for Freedom proposal embraced the following new features: (1) to make self-help an integral part of the food aid program; (2) to eliminate the "surplus" requirement for food aid; (3) to expand the magnitude of food aid shipments; and (4) to authorize the CCC to enrich nutritionally the foods shipped under the program. It would seem that the President had chosen to cope with the diminishing United States food surpluses by proposing a new program which constituted a shift toward foreign aid operations.

Johnson's proposal, however, was not the only one on future food aid to be considered by the second session of the Eighty-ninth Congress. A bill (S. 2157) to provide for United States participation and leadership in an international effort to end malnutrition and human want was introduced in the first session by Senator George S. Mc-

Govern and referred to the Committee on Foreign Relations. In the second session, this bill, at Senator McGovern's request, was discharged from the Committee on Foreign Relations and referred to the Committee on Agriculture and Forestry.

War on hunger

On January 19, 1966, Representative Harold D. Cooley, chairman of the House Committee on Agriculture, introduced a bill (H.R. 12152) which would wage world war on hunger and amend the Agricultural Trade Development and Assistance Act of 1954. Under the provisions of this bill, Titles I and II of the program would be extended until 1970 with an authorization of $2.5 billion annually for Title I and $800 million annually for Title II.

On January 26, Senator Mondale (D-Minnesota) introduced the World Hunger Act of 1966 (S. 2826). This bill called for three new actions: (1) a program of grants and low-interest loans to increase food and agricultural production in the recipient countries; (2) a program of grants of local currencies to finance various projects and programs including binational foundations; and (3) a program of loans, using CCC funds, to pay for transportation of Public Law 480 commodities to the recipient countries repayable in dollars within twenty years. The bill also proposed establishment of a cabinet-level policy council to assess needs for food and farm assistance in the less-developed countries.

The following day, January 27, Congressman Lynn E. Stalbaum (D-Wisconsin) submitted an amendment to Public Law 480 (H.R. 12375), calling for a reassessment of the United States role in the agricultural development of other nations, and including a provision for establishment of a rural peace corps.

On February 14, 1966, Representative Cooley, at the request of the Administration, introduced a bill (H.R. 12785) to promote international trade in agricultural commodities, to combat hunger and malnutrition, and to further economic development. This bill contained the provisions of the message to Congress by President Johnson on February 10. On the same day, Chairman Cooley also submitted a bill (H.R. 12784) to authorize the CCC to establish reserves of agricultural commodities to protect consumers, to meet the requirements of commercial exports, to fulfill the demands of the proposed Food for Freedom program, and to meet the requirements of the domestic relief programs.

Three days later, on February 17, Senator Ellender, by request, introduced the Administration's bill (S. 2933) on the Food for Freedom program in the Senate. Subsequently, the House Committee on Agriculture held hearings on H.R. 12152 and H.R. 12785 from January 14 to March 22, 1966.[4]

On the basis of evidence and testimony presented in these hearings, the committee collapsed many of the above provisions of the legislative proposals into a clean bill, H.R. 14929. This bill became the vehicle for the 1966 extension of Public Law 480. The Senate version of H.R. 14929, as initially passed, differed from the House version on some thirty-eight points. In conference, thirty-five Senate provisions and three House provisions were adopted. When the first conference report was considered by the House on September 5, Representative Belcher moved that the report be recommitted to conference on H.R. 14929 for further consideration. The point of contention was the Senate insistence on granting Presidential waiver to a prohibition of sales to recipient countries trading with North Vietnam or Cuba. Congressman Belcher's motion was accepted by a vote of 306 to 61 and the issue resolved in a second conference on H.R. 14929. As reported out of conference on October 18, the bill retains the outright prohibition as to countries trading with North Vietnam but permits the President to waiver the restriction as to countries dealing with Cuba if he finds it in the national interest to do so, and if the trade of such countries involves nothing except nonstrategic food and agricultural commodities, raw agricultural materials and medical supplies. Both Houses passed the second conference report on October 21, and the President signed it into law on November 11. The new law contains many new concepts which can make Food for Peace a revolutionary new program. Changes instigated by the new law confirm many of the findings of this study and shed light on future Food for Peace developments.

Utilization of non-surplus

Perhaps the most significant innovation is the utilization of non-surplus commodities. Food for Peace will no longer be based solely on surpluses, a change made obvious by the current lack of surplus agricultural commodities.

Wheat stocks on July 1 of this year [1966] amounted to only 536 million bushels. Corn stocks on October 1 are now estimated at only 950 million bushels and all food grains taken together only

47 million tons. When these low levels of carryover stocks are considered in relation to the population level that now exists in this country, both human and animal, it is evident that surpluses as such no longer exist.[5]

A second new concept limits Food for Peace shipments to commodities which recipient countries cannot obtain through their own resources. The third new concept makes United States assistance conditional on other wealthy nations' equitable participation in the war against hunger. A fourth new concept is to prevent the recurrence of new agricultural surpluses under the expanded farm policy program. The fifth concept calls for a more careful accounting and evaluation procedure to accompany future Food for Peace operations.

As signed into law on November 11, 1966, the new "Food for Peace Act" [Public Law 89-808] extended and amended Public Law 480. Title I of the new law combines previous Titles I and II by providing for sales both for foreign currencies and for dollars under long-term credit. The new Title II combines the foreign donation programs previously authorized under Titles II and III. Title III of the new law provides for the barter of agricultural commodities as carried on under previous legislation, while the new Title IV contains the general provisions and definitions of the program. By extending the Food for Peace program rather than individual titles for two years, the sale of commodities for dollars under long-term credit arrangements, previously a permanent program, has been made temporary. Congress authorized $1.9 billion per year plus carryover for the new Title I and $600 million per year plus carryover for the new Title II.

Several additional departures from the previous law should be noted. The most important substantive change is the elimination of the requirement that commodities must be designated as "surplus" before being eligible for shipment under Food for Peace programs. After consideration of domestic productive capacity, domestic requirements, farm and consumer price levels, and adequate carryover, the Secretary of Agriculture may—under the provisions of the new law— designate any United States agricultural commodities for Food for Peace utilization. However, he no longer has the authority to designate recipient countries. A second major change relates to self-help. Numerous provisions of the new law make continuation of Food for Peace assistance conditional on the recipient nations' progress toward a self-sufficient agricultural production. A third significant change in the program affects the priority among different forms of Food for Peace assistance. The President is specifically directed to conduct the program so as to assure a progressive transition (to be completed by 1971) from currency sales to either: (1) dollar sales, or (2) sales for currencies on terms so as to permit United States recovery of dollar credits from receipts.[6]

FUTURE EXECUTIVE-LEGISLATIVE INTERACTION

Although the 1966 extension and amendment of Public Law 480 constitutes a major departure from previous United States food aid programs, it failed to resolve the incipient new conflicts in Food for Peace. Perhaps it is for this reason that Congress extended the new program for only two years. Should this be the case, the next two years will be extremely critical for the future development of Food for Peace.

In the past, decisions affecting United States food aid policy have been strongly influenced by the Southern Democrats in the Agricultural Committee of the House and the Senate. As pointed out in Chapter III, the decision makers responding to the Executive request were primarily members of these two committees. One would, therefore, expect the Southern Democrats to play a key role in the formulation of food aid policy.

Shift toward sympathy

A first glance at the 1966 Senate Committee on Agriculture and Forestry[7] reveals a slight shift toward a more sympathetic attitude for the expansion of the foreign aid aspect of Public Law 480. Nevertheless, the Northern Democrats are still outnumbered by the Southern Democrat-Republican coalition four to one. The two most significant changes in the Senate committee are the increase of Presidential support from 47 to 53 percent and the increase from 35 to 40 percent in liberal members of the committee. Another meaningful change occurred with respect to the age of the committee. Now the Senators under fifty years old outnumber the Senators over seventy by 15 percent. Thus, it is no surprise that the Executive request emphasizing the foreign aid aspects of Food for Peace was met by the Senate Committee on Agriculture with unprecedented sympathy in 1966. Assuming that the composition of the Senate Committee on Agriculture and Forestry remains for all practical purposes unchanged, a rapport between the executive and the legislative branches of the government can be anticipated in 1968. Another significant reason for the continued amity between the executive and legislative branches of the government can be found in recent changes in the attitude of individual Southern Democratic senators toward the Food for Peace program. In Louisiana, for example, the rapid population shift from rural to urban has not only changed the nature of the state from farm to nonfarm, but has created new demands on the part of the constituency which are already reflected in representation before Congress. Similar transitions are taking place in many other Southern states.

The prospects for food assistance legislation will probably be determined within the context of three forces which led to the establishment of the Food for Peace program in 1961: (1) the world food problem; (2) the United States agricultural situation; and (3) the trends of United States foreign policy. Recent trends in these areas will delimit the Congressional response to any Executive request.

Food gap to widen

The projections of world population and food supply, presented in Chapter 2, indicate that the food gap will gradually widen throughout the remainder of the 1960's. At present there is no reason to question the validity of such projections, and therefore it is probable that the demand for food aid will increase rather than decrease. Will the United States continue to provide the bulk of such assistance? Secretary Freeman answers this question with a resounding, "No." In warning the underdeveloped nations not to expect continuation of unlimited food assistance from the United States, Freeman points out that by 1984—perhaps sooner—the capacity of the developed nations to feed the rest of the world will have been exhausted under a continuation of present circumstances. The changes incorporated in the Food for Peace program in 1966 reflect such thinking. There are, however, in the Congress three different factions, each of which offers a different solution to the dilemma. These groups—led by Senators Mc-Govern, Ellender, and Fulbright—can be expected to exert great influence on the course taken by Congress in the formulation of food aid policy.

Senator McGovern argues from the major premise that ". . . potential farm production in the absence of acreage diversion programs is increasing three times as fast today as thirty years ago, with most of the increase occurring in crop production per acre."[8] McGovern's minor premise is that food assistance to underdeveloped nations ". . . can contain the fires of unrest before they are kindled in the tinder of want. It is a far better weapon than a bomber in our competition with the communists for influence in the developing world."[9] The conclusion of Senator McGovern and his adherents is that expansion of our food aid program is not only in the domestic interest of the United States, but vital to the preservation of our national security.

Senator Ellender takes a more pessimistic view. He argues that the problem of world hunger cannot be permanently solved by American food aid and that the less-developed nations would rather spend their own resources on such things as steel mills, jet airplanes, and military adventures against their neighbors than on the improvement of their agricultural productivity.[10] Therefore, Ellender offers the following policy alternatives. The United States should gradually phase out large-scale food assistance. Recipients of United States food aid should be made to realize that assistance in the future will be subject to controls and supervision of agricultural development in their countries.[11]

A third point of view is presented by Senator Fulbright. By providing food aid in the absence of domestic surpluses, the Food for Peace program, according to Senator Fulbright, becomes out-and-out foreign aid.[12] Fulbright and his followers advocate an immediate and severe reduction of Food for Peace assistance as part of our foreign aid. While a continuation of assistance is considered by this group to be essential, they maintain it should be funneled through international lending institutions rather than provided on a bilateral basis by the United States government.

All three policy positions are reflected in the "Food for Peace Act of 1966." Each represents an embryo of the program's development in the future. Will one of these prevail over others, or will they coalesce around a new fourth policy position on United States food aid?

Chapter 8

Appendices

APPENDIX I

Summary by fiscal year and program
(U.S. Fiscal Years—Millions of Dollars)

U.S. overseas loans and grants—net obligations and loan authorizations

Program	Post-war relief period 1946-1948	Marshall Plan period 1949-1952	Mutual security act period 1953-1957	1958	1959	1960	1961	Foreign assistance act period 1962	1963	Total† 1946-1963	Repayments and interest 1946-1963	Total less repayments and interest
A.I.D. and predecessor agencies—total	—	14,505	9,140	1,620	1,916	1,866	2,012	2,508	2,296	35,868a	1,227	34,641
Loans	—	1,577	868	417	626	564	707	1,331	1,343	7,434	1,227	6,207
Grants	—	12,928	8,272	1,203	1,291	1,302	1,305	1,178	953	28,434	—	28,434
Social progress trust fund	—	—	—	—	—	—	—	224	125	349	1	348
Food for Peace—total	—	83	2,672	794	889	1,106	1,325	1,576	1,790	10,236	228	10,008
Title I—(total sales agreements)	(—)	(—)	(2,036)	(720)	(817)	(1,109)	(1,141)	(1,318)	(1,260)	(8,401)	(—)	(8,401)
Less: (planned for U.S. uses)	(—)	(—)	(569)	(312)	(216)	(237)	(297)	(241)	(192)	(2,065)	(—)	(2,065)
Title I—planned for loans and grants	—	—	1,467	408	601	872	844	1,077	1,068	6,336	228	6,108
104c—Grants for common defense	—	—	240	71	34	20	66	136	113	680	—	680
104e—Grants for economic development	—	—	210	25	100	317	260	302	302	1,517	—	1,517
104e—Loans to private industry	—	—	2	73	116	88	66	90	65	501	29	472
104g—Loans to government	—	—	1,016	239	350	447	452	548	588	3,639	199	3,440
Title I—ass't from other country sales agreements	—	—	37	5	—	—	—	—	15	57	1	56
Title II—emergency relief and economic development	—	—	317	87	48	63	242	176	306	1,239	—	1,239
Title III—voluntary relief agencies	—	83	850	295	240	172	240	271	325	2,475	—	2,475

APPENDIX I (continued)

U.S. overseas loans and grants—net obligations and loan authorizations

Program	Post-war relief period 1946-1948	Marshall Plan period 1949-1952	Mutual security act period					Foreign assistance act period		Total† 1946-1963	Repayments and interest 1946-1963	Total less repayments and interest
			1953-1957	1958	1959	1960	1961	1962	1963			
Title IV—dollar credit sales	–	–	–	–	–	–	–	52	76	128	°	128
Export-Import Bank long-term loans	2,096	904	1,510	518	711	305	962	535	572	8,111	4,759	3,352
Other U.S. economic programsᵇ	12,553	4,049	526	23	19	97	88	234	363	17,951	3,814	14,137
Total economic	14,649	19,541	13,847	2,956	3,535	3,374	4,388	5,077	5,146	72,515ᵃ	10,029	62,486
Loans	8,063	3,458	3,455	1,250	1,803	1,407	2,187	2,797	2,850	27,271	10,029	17,242
Grants	6,586	16,082	10,392	1,706	1,732	1,967	2,201	2,280	2,296	45,244	–	45,244
Military assistance program—(chg. to app.)ᶜ	–	2,517	14,863	2,363	2,110	1,718	1,374	1,448	1,810	30,528	216	30,312
(additional grants from excess stocks)	(–)	(513)	(448)	(257)	(197)	(289)	(328)	(248)	(188)	(2,584)	(–)	(2,584)
Other military assistance	481	324	444	41	50	127	88	78	24	1,659		1,659
Total military	481	2,842	15,307	2,404	2,160	1,845	1,462	1,526	1,834	32,187	216	31,971
Loans	–	–	15	39	60	21	30	21	45	416	216	200
Grants	481	2,842	15,293	2,366	2,101	1,824	1,432	1,505	1,789	31,771	–	31,771
Total economic and military	15,130	22,382	29,155	5,360	5,695	5,218	5,850	6,603	6,980	104,702	10,245	94,457
Loans	8,063	3,458	3,470	1,288	1,863	1,428	2,217	2,819	2,895	27,687	10,245	17,442
Grants	7,067	18,924	25,685	4,072	3,833	3,791	3,633	3,785	4,086	77,015	–	77,015

† See General Notes for coverage and qualifications, particularly for A.I.D. and for military programs.
° Less than $50,000.
ᵃ Includes $2 million not distributed by fiscal years.
ᵇ See page 141 for supplementary table on these programs.
ᶜ Annual data represent net deliveries. The cumulative total represents the total amount programmed for the period FY 1950-1963; and, therefore, the difference between the sum of the fiscal years and the cumulative total is the value of goods programmed but not yet delivered.

SOURCE: U.S. Congress, House Foreign Affairs Committee, *U.S. Overseas Loans and Grants and Assistance From International Organizations*, prepared by the Agency for International Development, March 30, 1964, p. 5.

APPENDIX II

The Executive Request: Secretary Freeman's Letter to the Congress[1]

Department of Agriculture
Washington, D.C., February 18, 1964

Hon. John W. McCormack
Speaker of the House of Representatives

Dear Mr. Speaker:

One of the deep satisfactions that come to me as Secretary of Agriculture is the fact that I am able to play a part in carrying forward our Nation's highly successful agricultural export program under Public Law 480. I know that many of my friends in Congress feel exactly the same way.

Public Law 480 currently is making a greater contribution than at any time in its nearly 10 years of operation. Shipments of U. S. agricultural products under the program reached an alltime high record of more than $1.6 billion, export market value, in calendar year 1963. Not only are such shipments putting food and fiber into the hands of needy foreign friends and accelerating their growth programs, but also they effectively serve our farm and business communities by building future foreign markets for our efficiently produced abundance. Hundreds of thousands of jobs on our farms and in our towns and cities depend wholly or substantially on the production, processing, transporting, and related activities brought about by Public Law 480.

The programs, operating in more than 100 nations, have begun to make a contribution to economic growth that is even more dramatic. More than half a million workers in 19 countries are paid directly in U. S. food under Public Law 480 food-for-work programs. Many thousands more are employed as a direct result of the use of local currencies for economic development projects.

Titles I and II of the Agricultural Trade Development and Assistance Act of 1954, as amended (Public Law 480, 83d Cong.) are authorized through the remainder of this calendar year. I am enclosing a draft of a proposed bill to extend these authorities.

It is proposed that (1) the authority to enter into agreements under title I be extended 5 calendar years through December 31, 1969, and increased by $7.1 billion for the 5-year period with a limitation of $2.5 billion in any calendar year with provision for the carryover of uncommitted authorizations from prior years, (2) the use of foreign currencies be authorized for procurement of equipment, materials, facilities, and services for internal security programs, in addition to the military categories presently authorized for the common defense, (3) the existing 25-percent limitation on loans to private business firms be eliminated, (4) authorization be included for the sale of title I currencies for dollars to voluntary agencies and to U. S.-flag vessels for payment of certain expenses incurred under the act, (5) the requirement of reports on activities under the act be changed from every 6 months to each year, and (6) the title II authority be increased to $450 million for each of the calendar years 1965 through 1969 and authority to make general average contributions be extended to title III, and related shipments.

Title I of Public Law 480 authorizes the President to enter into agreements with friendly nations or organizations of friendly nations to provide for the sale of surplus agricultural commodities for foreign currencies. Congressional authorizations for the 5-year period January 1, 1960, through December 31, 1964, total $9.5 billion, with a maximum of $2.5 billion during each of the calendar years 1961 through 1964. Programing for the past 5 years resulted in costs to the Commodity Credit Corporation of approximately $9 billion. However, it is anticipated that dollar reimbursements to the Commodity Credit Corporation from other agencies of the U. S. Government as a result of loan repayments and sales of title I currencies will provide approximately $1 billion so that authorization of further appropriations of $7.1 billion plus carryover of uncommitted authorizations will be sufficient. Public Law 87-128 which extended title I authority through December 31, 1964, did not include the provision for the carryover of uncommitted authorizations from prior years which had been included in previous extensions of title I. The enclosed draft of a proposed bill requests that this provision be restored to eliminate administrative and accounting problems which have resulted.

The request for a 5-year extension of the title I program is presented to permit continuation of orderly programming and shipment of agricultural surplus to food-and-fiber deficit areas of the world, principally less developed nations. Enactment of the proposal will facilitate efforts to make maximum utilization of our agricultural abundance under the food-for-peace program and to continue to negotiate agreements on a long-term basis where there are opportunities to program commodities and it is in the interest of American agriculture to do so.

The foreign currency uses now include authorization for procurement of military equipment, materials, facilities, and services for the common defense. In order to make clear that this authority can be used for activities in support of counterinsurgency programs, such as the Vietnam strategic hamlet program, and other activities vital to counteract Communist-inspired subversion and insurgency, we are requesting that the authority be changed to delete reference to "military" goods and services and to make explicit that the authority may be used to procure any goods and services necessary for the common defense, including within that concept internal security programs.

Public Law 480 now provides a limit of 25 percent on the amount of foreign currency that can be set aside in each agreement for loans to private business firms. There may be occasions when it would be beneficial to the developing countries and to the United States to provide for a larger share of title I currency for this purpose.

Amendment of section 104 is requested to provide for the sale of title I foreign currencies to U. S. voluntary agencies for use in paying expenses abroad in connection with the distribution of donated commodities and to U. S.-flag vessels for use in paying port fees, unloading, lightering, and other charges at destination in connection with the carrying of Public Law 480 cargo. It is now necessary for these users to purchase foreign currencies abroad to pay these expenses, and the sale of title I currencies for this purpose would represent a dollar saving to the United States in countries where it is not necessary to purchase currencies to meet other U. S. obligations. This amendment would facilitate the negotiation of agreements providing for the use of funds for these purposes.

The act provides that a report on activities be made every 6 months. The 19th semiannual report now in preparation, as well as the several immediately preceding reports, reveal that these summaries of statistics and factual information will serve the purpose at considerably lower cost if they are submitted annually. Additional timely information is made available to the committees, Congress, and the public as it becomes available and is most useful.

In order to permit continuation of useful activities which have been possible under title II of Public Law 480 (relating to famine relief and other assistance), it is proposed that this authority be extended for 5 calendar years through December 31, 1969. It is also proposed that the authorization be increased to $450 million per calendar year. This amount, along with uncommitted authorizations from prior years, will provide for an expansion in the economic and community development programs authorized under section 202. The current authorization for title II programs is $300 million per calendar year. However, by utilizing uncommitted authorizations from prior years, programing for fiscal year 1963 was at a rate of $354 million. Section 203 of Public Law 480 also authorizes the use of title II funds to pay certain transportation costs on commodities donated under section 416 of the Agricultural Act of 1949, as amended, and authorizes the payment of charges for general average contributions from title II funds. It is proposed that language be inserted to extend the authority for the payment of charges for general average contributions to commodities donated under section 416 and related statutes when title II funds are used to pay ocean freight charges.

With the possible exception of the increasing operations under title II, enactment of the proposed legislation would result in no increase in employment or administrative costs in the fiscal year 1965. The program cost of $1.5 billion estimated for the fiscal year 1965 takes into account the proposed amendments.

The Bureau of the Budget advises that enactment of the proposed legislation would be in accord with the program of the President.

A similar letter is being sent to the President of the Senate.

Sincerely yours,
Orville L. Freeman
Secretary

APPENDIX III

Chronology, Issues, and Provisions of the 1964 Extension and Amendment of Public Law 480

This appendix summarizes twenty-eight issues of the 1964 extension and amendment of Public Law 480 during eight different time periods of the legislative process: (1) the Executive request for Public Law 480 legislation which was made on February 18, 1964;[1] (2) the Senate bill (S. 2687) as introduced by Senator Ellender on March 25, 1964;[2] (3) the Senate bill as reported out of committee on August 18, 1964;[3] (4) the Senate bill as passed on the floor of the Senate on August 19, 1964;[4] (5) the House bill (H.R. 12298) as introduced on August 7, 1964 by Representative Poage;[5] (6) the House bill as reported out of committee on August 11, 1964;[6] (7) the House bill as passed on the floor of the House on September 3, 1964;[7] and (8) the provisions of the final law as written by the conference committee and approved by the President on October 8, 1964.[8] The final law (Public Law 88-638) modified Public Law 480 on 23 counts.[9]

1. *The Period of Extension for Title I*. Public Law 88-638 provided for a two-year extension of Title I of Public Law 480.[10] There were serious differences among the legislative participants with respect to the period of extension prior to conference. The House bill contained provision for a three-year extension as introduced,[11] reported,[12] and passed on the floor.[13] The Senate bill, as introduced,[14] incorporated the five-year extension period for Title I as requested by Secretary Freeman;[15] in committee, however, the Senate provision for the extension of Title I was reduced to two years,[16] and this provision remained in the Senate bill as passed on the floor.[17]

2. *The Period for Extension of Title II*. The situation with respect to Title II was identical to that of Title I at all levels of the legislative process.[18]

3. *The Amount of Funds Authorized for Title I*. The final provision for the extension and amendment of Public Law 480 authorized funding for new Title I agreements in the amount of $2.7 billion for the two-year period of extension; provision was included, however, to raise this amount by carrying over any unused funds from previous authorizations (a provision which was not included in the 1961 extension and amendment) and by permitting the funds paid to the CCC in reimbursement for currency use by other government agencies to be used for new agreements.[19] As in the case of the issue involving the period of extension, there were serious differences at various stages in the legislative process. The House provision remained at a constant $4 billion authorization, plus provision for carryover, from introduction through passage on the floor.[20] In accord with the Executive request,[21] the Senate bill, as introduced, contained provision for authoriza-

tion of $7.5 billion plus carryover for a five-year period, stipulating, however, a limitation of $2.5 billion on agreements signed during any one year.[22] The Senate Committee on Agriculture and Forestry made a serious revision with respect to the total amount of authorization, reducing it to $2.7 billion for a two-year period, plus carryover, with the $2.5-billion limitation.[23] This provision was retained in the Senate bill as passed on the floor[24] and was adopted by the conference committee. In terms of the total amounts, these differences appear larger than they actually were because of the different time periods involved. When these authorizations are adjusted for the time period over which the funds were to be spent, however, significant differences remain. The authorization, as requested by the Executive and incorporated into the Senate bill, as introduced, amounted to $1.5 billion per year plus carryover; the later Senate provision and the final law reduced the yearly authorization to $1.35 billion plus carryover; and the House provision dropped the average annual amount to $1.33 billion and did not provide for carryover.

4. *The Amount of Funds Authorized for Title II*. The final law provided an annual Title II authorization of $400 million plus carryover (a provision contained in the 1961 extension and amendment) for each of the two years.[25] Unlike the situation with respect to Title I, House provisions for Title II were more permissive, stipulating annual authorizations of $400 million plus carryover.[26] This annual amount corresponded with the annual amount requested by the Executive,[27] as did the Senate provision when introduced.[28] In the Senate committee, however, the Title II authorization was reduced to the annual amount of $375 million plus carryover,[29] and an identical measure was passed on the floor of the Senate.[30]

5. *Sales to Communist Countries and Nations Trading with Castro's Cuba*. A provision of the final law prohibited Title I sales to any communist country (i.e., Poland and Yugoslavia) or to any country whose ships or aircraft were permitted to trade with Cuba. This same provision stipulated, however, that such countries would be eligible for Title IV sales, and countries otherwise ineligible because of the Battle Act were restricted to five-year credit.[31] As will be discussed later, the cessation of aid to Poland and Yugoslavia was one of the major issues on the floor of the House of Representatives. Opponents of the prohibition managed to defeat it on the floor, but it was reinserted by the conference committee. The provision excluding nations trading with Castro's Cuba from Title I programs originated as a House-floor amendment redefining the concept of "friendly nations."[32]

6. *Public Law 480 Sales to "Aggressor Nations."* The 1964 extension and amendment changed Public Law 480 so as to prohibit Title I and IV sales to any nations which the President determined to be either: (1) an aggressor nation with respect to any friendly nation having diplomatic re-

lations with the United States, or (2) using funds obtained from the United States for purposes inimical to the United States interest.[33] This was another issue raised on the floor of the House of Representatives and, as in the case of sales to communist nations, the formal proposals do not convey the seriousness of Congressional concern. As it arose, this provision was directed specifically toward the United Arab Republic (UAR), and there was serious consideration of excluding the UAR from Public Law 480 programs by name. The discussion in the House produced a provision identical to that of the final law, except in one important respect: before providing Public Law 480 assistance to any nation, according to the House provision, the President was required to determine that such nation was neither an aggressor nation nor using United States funds for purposes inimical to interests of the United States.[34] The action on the part of the conference committee, therefore, effectively pulled the teeth of the House proposal.

7.*Limitation on United States Financing of Ocean Freight Charges.* The provisions of the final law, resulting from the 1964 extension and amendment, severely restricted the authority of agencies administering Public Law 480 programs to finance ocean freight charges on food shipments.[35] Prior to 1964, rather extensive authority had existed for payment of such costs related to Food-for-Peace shipments either as outright United States financing or, in some instances, with the United States receiving payments from the recipient countries for shipping costs in the form of foreign currencies. The 1964 provision stipulated that with respect to all agreements signed after January 1, 1965, payment by the United States of Public Law 480 ocean freight costs would be restricted to the differential resulting from the Cargo Preference Act; further, payment of the balance by the recipient must be in dollars. It has been estimated that this provision doubles the foreign exchange which recipient nations need for this purpose.[36] The origin of this provision was in the Senate bill as introduced[37] and no change was made in committee[38] or on the floor.[39]

8.*Exchange Rates for Title I Sales.* Expressing Congressional concern of long standing over the concessional nature of Title I, the final law specified that the exchange rates for Title I sales must be the highest legally obtainable and in no instance less favorable than those obtained by any other nation.[40] The issue of exchange rates of Title I sales originated in the Senate bill as introduced. This bill provided that presidential reports on Public Law 480 activities specify Title I, II, and IV exchange rates obtained in agreements, make estimates as to the real values of foreign currencies involved, and justify accepted rates.[41] The House bill, as introduced, contained a provision identical to that of the final law;[42] the Senate adopted the House proposal in committee.[43] The House provision remained in both bills hereafter.[44]

9.*The Executive-Legislative Advisory Committee.* Another issue, which this discussion does not present in its full complexity, was the provision established by the 1964 extension and amendment for an Executive-Legislative Advisory Committee.[45] As spelled out in the law, this committee is composed of the Secretary of Agriculture, the director of the Bureau of the Budget, the administrator of the Agency for International Development, the chairman and ranking minority member of the House Committee on Agriculture, and the chairman and ranking minority member of the Senate Committee on Agriculture and Forestry. This committee is to review the status of foreign currencies from time to time and make recommendations to the President concerning: (1) the use of such currencies, and (2) obtaining maximum returns from Title I sales. Furthermore, the President is directed to consult this committee with respect to: (1) policies relating to existing provisions for disposal of Title I currencies, and (2) certain interest rates under Title IV. The idea of such a committee with the former two powers of recommendation originated in the House bill as introduced;[46] this provision was left unchanged in committee.[47] After extended discussion on the floor of the House, opponents of the measure managed to amend it out of the final House bill,[48] only to have the conference committee reinsert the measure in more stringent form.

10. *Congressional Approval of Title I Grants and Loans.* Closely related to the item just discussed was a provision which was not incorporated into any document prior to the final law—this was the stipulation that any proposed grants of Title I currencies (with the exception of grants for military purposes) must be submitted to the House and Senate Committees on Agriculture with either committee having the right of disapproval.[49]

11. *The Amount of Title I Currencies Subject to the Appropriations Process.* A third provision, whereby Congress expressed its disapproval of existing policies regarding the use of Title I currencies, raised the amount of Title I currencies subject to the appropriations process from 10 to 20 percent of the holdings of such funds.[50] This provision was first inserted by the Senate committee,[51] later picked up by the House bill as introduced,[52] and retained thereafter in all bills throughout the rest of the legislative process.[53]

12. *The Convertibility of Foreign Currencies.* The concern of Congress, with respect to the inability of the United States to use Title I currencies to the maximum extent, emerged as a provision of the final law that Title I currencies must be convertible to the extent ". . . consistent with the purposes of the Act" and, in any event, such currencies must be convertible to such an extent as necessary to pay the obligations of United States agencies in recipient nations.[54] To a large extent, this measure was directed toward the United Arab Republic where, despite large United States currency holdings, Title I agreements had specified that such currencies could not be used to pay United States toll charges in the Suez Canal. The issue of convertibility was first raised by the Senate bill as introduced, which specified that Title I currencies should be convertible to the extent consistent

with the purposes of the Act.[55] This provision was modified in committee by the stipulation that United States uses of Title I currencies must not be restricted at all by Title I agreements.[56] While the committee provision was passed on the floor of the Senate,[57] the conference committee toned down the wording of the final law.

13.*Interest Rates on Title IV Loans.* The final law requires that Title IV loans bear a rate of interest not less than that required under the Foreign Assistance Act, i.e., one percent for up to ten years and two and one-half percent thereafter.[58] This provision originated with the Senate bill, as introduced, which was identical with the stipulation of the final law.[59] In the Senate committee[60] and as passed on the floor[61] of the Senate, the language of the Senate provision was changed slightly.

14.*Interest Rates on Title I Loans.* A further stipulation of the final law dealing with interest rates specifies that Title I agreements, signed after January 1, 1965, must bear a rate of interest not less than the cost of funds to the United States Treasury, unless a lower rate is recommended by the advisory committee.[62] This provision originated with the Senate bill, as introduced,[63] and was retained without change by the Senate.[64]

15.*Use of Title II Funds to Purchase Title I Currencies.* A provision of the final law authorized the use of $7.5 million of CCC funds under Title II for the purchase of Title I currencies to be used in the support of food donation programs. With the exception of a minor change in committee,[65] the House originated and passed this provision without a limitation on the amount of funds to be used.[66]

16.*Cooley Loan Limitations.* The Executive request asked that the previous limitation of 25 percent on Title I currencies, which could be used for loans to private enterprise in recipient countries, be removed.[67] Such a provision was inserted in all documents under consideration,[68] with one exception: on the floor of the House, this provision was amended out of the House bill.[69]

17.*Sales of Title I Currencies to United States Citizens.* Under the authority of Public Law 88-638, Section 416B of the Foreign Assistance Act of 1961 was incorporated into Public Law 480; in effect, this permitted the sale of Title I currencies to United States citizens for travel and other purposes.[70] This provision originated with the House bill as introduced,[71] and was subsequently inserted in both the House and Senate bills during the remainder of the legislative process.[72]

18.*Use of Title I Currencies for Internal Security Programs in Recipient Countries.* Of the Executive requests, only this item and one other were accepted without revision by Congress. Under the terms of the Executive request, the final law authorized the use of Title I currencies in support of internal security (counterinsurgency) programs in recipient countries.[73] The same provision was included in all drafts of the 1964 extension and amendment.[74]

19.*General Average Contributions.* The Executive request that authority to pay general average contributions on shipments of Public Law 480 commodities be extended to Title III Section 416 programs, was incorporated into all drafts of the House and Senate bills as well as the final law.[75] As such, this was the second of the Executive requests adopted without change by Congress.

20.*Communist China.* The law provided that Title I funds should be used for the purpose of assisting nations friendly with the United States to remain independent of trade with Communist China; this merely included Communist China under an existing portion of the law which previously referred only to the USSR.[76] Different provisions directed toward the same end were inserted on the floor of the House and the Senate; the floor amendment of the Senate bill was the one incorporated into the final law,[77] while the House amendment, which included Communist China among those nations unfriendly to the United States,[78] was omitted in conference.

21.*Annual Presidential Reports.* The Executive request asked that the previously semiannual reports on activities carried on under Public Law 480 be made annual.[79] With the above noted exception (under item #8) of the Senate stipulation that such reports provide extensive detail with respect to Title I exchange rates.[80] This request was accepted without modification by Congress.[81]

22.*Use of Title III Commodities for Self-Help Activities.* A provision of the final law changed Title III of Public Law 480 so as to permit the use of such commodities for self-help programs in recipient nations, so long as such programs were designed to alleviate the need for such assistance.[82] This provision originated in the House bill as introduced and was not changed subsequently.[83]

23.*Public Law 480 Classified as Expenditure for International Affairs and Finance in the Budget.* A final[84] modification made by the 1964 extension and amendment in Public Law 480 was the stipulation that expenditures under the program should be classified as expenditures for "international affairs and finance," rather than expenditures for agriculture in the budget.[85] This provision originated in the Senate committee[86] and was retained on the floor of the Senate.[87]

In terms of the present discussion, five other issues are of interest. While the following five issues (numbered consecutively for future reference) were not incorporated into the final law, they were incorporated into the drafts of various bills for the extension and amendment.

24.*Sale of Title I Currencies to Voluntary Agencies.* It was originally proposed in the Executive request that permission be granted for the sale of Title I currencies to voluntary agencies for use in recipient countries under Title II and III programs.[88] This provision was included in the Senate bill as introduced[89] but was deleted in committee and never revived.

25.*Sale of Title I Currencies to U. S.-Flag Vessels.* The Executive request proposed that provision be made for the sale of Title I currencies to United States shippers participating in the program; these currencies would then be used for payment of unloading costs, port fees, etc. in recipient countries.[90] This item was also included in the Senate bill as introduced,[91] subsequently deleted, and never reinserted.

26.*Use of Title I Currencies for Self-Help Projects.* A proposal was contained in the House bill as introduced which would have permitted use of Title I currencies in recipient countries for training programs in the skills necessary for economic development.[92] This provision was modified slightly in committee[93] and deleted on the floor of the House; it was never reintroduced.

27.*Use of Title I Currencies for Congressional Investigation.* A proposal was inserted in the House bill as introduced which authorized the use of Title I currencies by the House and Senate Agricultural Committees in connection with the investigation of the operations of the program.[94] This provision was deleted in committee and not revived.

28.*Prohibition of Use of Title I Currencies to Develop Recipient Competition with United States Agriculture.* An amendment was passed on the floor of the House which prohibited the use of Title I currencies, within recipient nations, for development purposes which would have the result of increasing competition with the normal agricultural exports of the United States.[95] This provision was dropped by the conference committee.

APPENDIX IV

Roll-Call Votes in the House of Representatives

1. HR 12298. Agriculture Trade Development and Assistance Act of 1954 (PL 480). Findley (R-Ill.) motion to recommit the bill with instruction to add an amendment prohibiting sale of surplus U.S. farm goods under Title I of PL 480 to nations controlled or dominated by a Communist government or—as under existing law—by "the world Communist movement." (The amendment was aimed at Poland and Yugoslavia.) Accepted 183-175: R 143-13; D 40-162 (ND 6-108; SD 34-54), Sept. 3, 1964. A "nay" was a vote supporting the President's position.

9. HR 12298. Passage of the bill extending PL 480 for three years, through Dec. 31, 1967, and authorizing the commitment of up to $4 billion for Title I over the three years, plus the use of unused previous authorizations, and $450 million annually for Title II, plus unused previous authorizations. Passed 349-6: R 151-4; D 198-2 (ND 112-0; SD 86-2), Sept. 3, 1964. A "yea" was a vote supporting the President's position.

KEY TO ROLL-CALL VOTES

Y Record Vote For (yea).
V Paired For.
‡ Announced For, CQ Poll For.
N Record Vote Against (nay).
X Paired Against.
— Announced Against, CQ Poll Against.
P Absent, General Pair, "Present," Did not announce or answer Poll.
Democrats in this type; *Republicans in italics.*

SOURCE: *Congressional Quarterly Almanac,* vol. xx, 1964, pp. 656-57.

APPENDIX IV (continued)

District & Name	1.	9.
ALABAMA		
AL Andrews	√	?
AL Elliott	N	Y
AL Grant	√	?
AL Huddleston	Y	Y
AL Jones	N	Y
AL Rains	?	?
AL Roberts	Y	Y
AL Selden	Y	Y
ALASKA		
AL Rivers	N	Y
ARIZONA		
3 Senner	N	Y
2 Udall	N	Y
1 Rhodes	Y	Y
ARKANSAS		
1 Gathings	N	Y
4 Harris	N	Y
2 Mills	N	Y
3 Trimble	N	Y
CALIFORNIA		
5 Burton	N	Y
7 Cohelon	N	Y
9 Edwards	N	Y
18 Hagen	N	Y
34 Hanna	X	?
2 Johnson	N	Y
4 Leggett	N	Y
15 McFall	N	Y
8 Miller	N	Y
3 Moss	–	‡
33 Sheppard	N	Y
16 Sisk	N	Y
37 Van Deerlin	Y	Y
14 Baldwin	Y	Y
1 Clausen	Y	Y
10 Gubser	Y	Y
6 Mailliard	√	?
38 Martin	Y	Y
12 Talcott	Y	Y
13 Teague	Y	Y
35 Utt	Y	Y
36 Wilson	Y	Y
11 Younger	Y	Y
Los Angeles Co.		
29 Brown	N	Y
27 Burkhalter	?	?
25 Cameron	N	Y
22 Corman	N	Y
21 Hawkins	N	Y
19 Holifield	N	Y
17 King	N	Y
26 Roosevelt	N	Y
30 Roybal	N	Y
31 Wilson	?	?
28 Bell	Y	Y
23 Clauson	Y	Y
32 Hosmer	Y	Y
24 Lipscomb	Y	Y
20 Smith	Y	Y
COLORADO		
4 Aspinall	N	Y
1 Rogers	N	‡
2 Brotzman	Y	Y
3 Chenoweth	Y	Y
CONNECTICUT		
1 Daddario	N	Y
3 Giaimo	N	Y
AL Grabowski	N	Y
5 Monagan	X	‡
2 St. Onge	N	Y
4 Sibal	Y	Y
DELAWARE		
AL McDowell	N	Y
FLORIDA		
2 Bennett	Y	Y
4 Fascell	N	Y
9 Fuqua	Y	Y
10 Gibbons	Y	Y
7 Haley	Y	Y
5 Herlong	X	‡
8 Matthews	N	Y
3 Pepper	N	Y
6 Rogers	Y	Y
1 Sikes	Y	Y
12 Cramer	√	‡
11 Gurney	Y	Y
GEORGIA		
7 Davis	N	Y
4 Flynt	?	?
3 Forrester	?	?
1 Hagan	N	Y

APPENDIX IV (continued)

	1.	9.
9 Landrum	?	?
2 Pilcher	?	?
10 Stephens	‡	‡
8 Tuten	N	Y
6 Vinson	N	Y
5 Weltner	Y	Y
HAWAII		
AL Gill	X	‡
AL Matsunaga	X	‡
IDAHO		
2 Harding	N	Y
1 White	X	Y
ILLINOIS		
21 Gray	N	‡
24 Price	X	?
23 Shipley	√	‡
16 Anderson	√	‡
17 Arends	Y	Y
20 Findley	√	?
14 Hoffman	√	‡
12 McClory	√	Y
19 McLoskey	Y	Y
18 Michel	Y	Y
15 Reid	Y	Y
22 Springer	Y	Y

	1.	9.
CHICAGO—COOK Co.		
1 Dawson	?	?
9 Finnegan	?	?
5 Kluczynski	X	?
7 Libonati	N	Y
3 Murphy	N	Y
6 Vacancy		
2 O'Hara	N	Y
11 Pucinski	N	Y
8 Rostenkowski	N	Y
10 Collier	Y	Y
4 Derwinski	Y	Y
13 Rumsfeld	Y	Y
INDIANA		
3 Brademas	N	Y
8 Denton	N	Y
1 Madden	N	Y
5 Roush	N	Y
4 Adair	Y	Y
7 Bray	Y	Y
11 Bruce	Y	Y
2 Halleck	Y	Y
10 Harvey	?	√
6 Roudebush	Y	Y
9 Wilson	Y	Y

	1.	9.
IOWA		
5 Smith	N	Y
2 Bromwell	Y	Y
3 Gross	Y	Y
6 Hoeven	Y	Y
7 Jensen	Y	Y
4 Kyl	Y	Y
1 Schwengel	Y	Y
KANSAS		
2 Avery	?	?
1 Dole	Y	Y
3 Ellsworth	N	Y
4 Shriver	N	Y
5 Skubitz	N	Y
KENTUCKY		
4 Chelf	N	Y
2 Natcher	N	Y
7 Perkins	N	Y
1 Stubblefield	N	Y
6 Watts	N	Y
5 Siler	N	Y
3 Snyder	Y	Y
LOUISIANA		
2 Boggs	N	Y

	1.	9.
1 Hebert	√	√
8 Long	N	Y
6 Morrison	N	Y
5 Passman	Y	N
7 Thompson	N	Y
4 Waggonner	Y	Y
3 Willis	N	Y
MAINE		
2 McIntire	?	?
1 Tupper	?	?
MARYLAND		
4 Fallon	N	Y
7 Friedel	N	Y
3 Garmatz	N	Y
5 Lankford	N	Y
2 Long	N	Y
AL Sickles	N	Y
6 Mathias	N	Y
1 Morton	Y	Y
MASSACHUSETTS		
2 Boland	X	‡
11 Burke	N	Y
4 Donohue	N	Y
7 Macdonald	N	Y
9 McCormack	N	

APPENDIX IV (continued)

	1.	9.
8 O'Neill	N	Y
3 Philbin	N	Y
6 Bates	∨	Y
1 Conte	Y	Y
12 Keith	Y	Y
10 Martin	?	?
5 Morse	N	Y
MICHIGAN		
7 O'Hara	N	Y
AL Staebler	N	Y
12 Vacancy		
18 Broomfield	Y	Y
10 Cederberg	Y	Y
6 Chamberlain	Y	Y
5 Ford	Y	Y
9 Griffin	Y	Y
8 Harvey	?	?
4 Hutchinson	Y	Y
3 Johansen	Y	Y
11 Knox	Y	Y
2 Meader	∨	?
DETROIT—WAYNE CO.		
13 Diggs	-	‡
15 Dingell	?	?
17 Griffiths	∨	X

	1.	9.
16 Lesinski	?	?
1 Nedzi	?	?
14 Ryan	-	‡
MINNESOTA		
8 Blatnik	N	Y
5 Fraser	N	Y
4 Karth	N	Y
6 Olson	N	‡
7 Langen	Y	Y
3 MacGregor	Y	‡
2 Nelsen	Y	Y
1 Quie	Y	Y
MISSISSIPPI		
1 Abernethy	Y	Y
5 Colmer	∨	?
2 Whitten	Y	Y
3 Williams	Y	Y
4 Winstead	Y	Y
MISSOURI		
5 Bolling	-	
9 Vacancy		
6 Hull	Y	Y
8 Ichord	Y	Y
10 Jones	N	Y

	1.	9.
1 Karsten	N	Y
4 Randall	N	Y
3 Sullivan	Y	Y
2 Curtis	Y	N
7 Hall	Y	Y
MONTANA		
1 Olsen	N	Y
2 Battin	Y	Y
NEBRASKA		
1 Beermann	Y	Y
2 Cunningham	Y	Y
3 Martin	Y	Y
NEVADA		
AL Baring	?	?
NEW HAMPSHIRE		
2 Cleveland	Y	Y
1 Wyman	Y	Y
NEW JERSEY		
14 Daniels	N	Y
13 Gallagher	N	Y
8 Joelson	N	Y
11 Minish	N	Y
15 Patten	N	Y

	1.	9.
10 Rodino	N	Y
4 Thompson	N	Y
3 Auchincloss	Y	Y
1 Cahill	Y	Y
6 Dwyer	Y	Y
5 Frelinghuysen	Y	Y
2 Glenn	Y	Y
9 Osmers	N	Y
12 Wallhauser	?	?
7 Widnall	Y	Y
NEW MEXICO		
AL Montoya	‡	‡
AL Morris	‡	‡
NEW YORK		
41 Dulski	N	Y
29 O'Brien	N	Y
1 Pike	N	Y
35 Stratton	X	‡
25 Barry	∨	X
5 Becker	Y	Y
3 Derounian	Y	Y
38 Goodell	Y	Y
2 Grover	Y	Y
36 Horton	Y	Y
31 Kilburn	∨	‡

APPENDIX IV (continued)

No. Name	1.	9.
30 King	Y	Y
40 Miller	?	?
37 Ostertag	Y	?
39 Pillion	√	?
32 Pirnie	Y	Y
26 Reid	N	Y
34 Riehlman	Y	Y
33 Robison	Y	Y
27 St. George	Y	Y
28 Wharton	Y	Y
4 Wydler	Y	Y
NEW YORK CITY		
7 Addabbo	N	N
23 Buckley	?	?
15 Carey	N	N
10 Celler	X	?
9 Delaney	N	Y
19 Farbstein	N	Y
22 Gilbert	N	Y
21 Healey	-	‡
12 Kelly	N	Y
11 Keogh	X	√
13 Multer	X	‡
16 Murphy	N	Y
18 Powell	N	Y
14 Rooney	N	Y
8 Rosenthal	N	Y
20 Ryan	N	Y
24 Fino	N	Y
6 Halpern	N	Y
17 Lindsay	N	Y
NORTH CAROLINA		
1 Bonner	N	Y
4 Cooley	N	Y
2 Fountain	Y	Y
3 Henderson	Y	Y
6 Kornegay	√	?
7 Lennon	Y	Y
5 Scott	Y	Y
11 Taylor	Y	Y
10 Whitener	Y	Y
9 Broyhill	Y	Y
8 Jonas	Y	Y
NORTH DAKOTA		
1 Andrews	N	Y
2 Short	Y	Y
OHIO		
9 Ashley	N	Y
20 Feighan	Y	Y
18 Hays	X	‡
19 Kirwan	N	Y
15 Secrest	Y	Y
21 Vanik	N	Y
10 Abele	Y	Y
17 Ashbrook	Y	Y
14 Ayres	Y	Y
8 Betts	Y	Y
22 Bolton, F. P.	Y	Y
11 Bolton, O. P.	Y	Y
16 Bow	Y	Y
7 Brown	Y	Y
2 Clancy	Y	Y
12 Devine	Y	Y
6 Harsha	Y	Y
5 Latta	Y	Y
4 McCulloch	√	?
23 Minshall	Y	Y
13 Mosher	Y	Y
1 Rich	Y	Y
3 Schenck	Y	Y
AL Taft	Y	Y
OKLAHOMA		
3 Albert	N	N
2 Edmondson	N	Y
5 Jarman	Y	Y
4 Steed	N	Y
6 Wickersham	N	Y
1 Belcher	Y	Y
OREGON		
4 Duncan	N	Y
3 Green	-	‡
2 Ullman	N	Y
1 Norblad	Y	Y
PENNSYLVANIA		
25 Clark	N	Y
21 Dent	N	Y
11 Flood	N	Y
20 Holland	N	Y
14 Moorhead	N	‡
26 Morgan	N	Y
6 Rhodes	√	?
15 Rooney	N	Y
18 Corbett	N	Y
8 Curtin	Y	Y
9 Dague	Y	Y
27 Fulton	Y	Y
19 Gooding	Y	Y
23 Johnson	Y	Y
16 Kunkel	Y	Y
10 McDade	Y	Y
7 Milliken	Y	Y

APPENDIX IV (continued)

District / Name	1.	9.
22 Saylor	Y	Y
17 Schneebeli	Y	Y
13 Schweiker	Y	Y
24 Weaver	Y	Y
12 Whalley	Y	Y
PHILADELPHIA CITY		
1 Barrett	N	N
3 Byrne	N	Y
5 Green	N	Y
2 Nix	N	Y
4 Toll	X	‡
RHODE ISLAND		
2 Fogarty	N	Y
1 St. Germain	N	Y
SOUTH CAROLINA		
4 Ashmore	Y	Y
3 Dorn	Y	N
5 Vacancy		
6 McMillan	N	Y
1 Rivers	N	Y
2 Watson	Y	Y
SOUTH DAKOTA		
2 Berry	Y	Y
1 Reifel	Y	Y
TENNESSEE		
6 Bass	N	Y
9 Davis	N	N
8 Everett	N	N
4 Evins	?	‡
5 Fulton	X	‡
7 Murray	N	Y
2 Baker	Y	Y
3 Brock	Y	Y
1 Quillen	Y	N
TEXAS		
3 Beckworth	N	Y
2 Brooks	N	Y
17 Burleson	N	Y
22 Casey	Y	Y
7 Dowdy	Y	Y
21 Fisher	Y	Y
20 Gonzalez	N	Y
15 Kilgore	‡	‡
19 Mahon	N	Y
1 Patman	N	Y
10 Pickle	N	Y
11 Poage	N	Y
AL Pool	N	Y
13 Purcell	–	Y
4 Roberts	N	Y
18 Rogers	Y	Y
6 Teague	N	Y
8 Thomas	N	Y
9 Thompson	N	Y
12 Wright	N	?
14 Young	N	Y
5 Alger	∨	?
16 Foreman	Y	N
UTAH		
1 Burton	Y	Y
2 Lloyd	Y	Y
VERMONT		
AL Stafford	Y	Y
VIRGINIA		
4 Abbitt	Y	Y
1 Downing	N	N
3 Gary	N	Y
2 Hardy	N	Y
9 Jennings	Y	Y
7 Marsh	Y	Y
8 Smith	N	Y
5 Tuck	Y	Y
10 Broyhill	Y	Y
6 Poff	Y	Y
WASHINGTON		
3 Hansen	X	‡
5 Horan	N	Y
4 May	Y	Y
1 Pelly	Y	X
7 Stinson	Y	N
6 Tollefson	Y	Y
2 Westland	Y	Y
WEST VIRGINIA		
4 Hechler	N	Y
5 Kee	?	‡
3 Slack	N	Y
2 Staggers	Y	Y
1 Moore	Y	Y
WISCONSIN		
9 Johnson	N	Y
2 Kastenmeier	N	Y
5 Reuss	X	‡
4 Zablocki	N	Y
8 Byrnes	Y	Y
7 Laird	Y	Y
10 O'Konski	Y	Y
1 Schadeberg	Y	Y
3 Thomson	Y	Y
6 Van Pelt	Y	Y
WYOMING		
AL Harrison	Y	Y

APPENDIX V

Roll-Call Votes in the Senate

1. S 2687. Extend and amend the Agricultural Trade Development and Assistance Act of 1954 (PL 480). Fulbright (D-Ark.) motion to send the conference report on S 2687 (see below) to the Senate Foreign Relations Committee for study with instructions to report the bill back to the Senate with recommendations by Sept. 30. Rejected 24-46. R 5-20; D 19-26 (ND 14-15; SD 5-11), Sept. 24, 1964. The President did not take a position on the motion.

10. S 2687. Adoption of the conference report (H Rept 1897) on the bill extending PL 480 for two years, through 1966, and making major changes in the law including the halting of sales of surplus U.S. farm goods to Poland and Yugoslavia for the currencies of those nations. Adopted 54-11: R 24-0; D 30-11 (ND 16-9; SD 14-2), Sept. 24, 1964. A "yea" was a vote supporting the President's position.

KEY TO ROLL-CALL VOTES

Y Record Vote For (yea).
V Paired For.
‡ Announced For, CQ Poll For.
N Record Vote Against (nay).
X Paired Against.
– Announced Against, CQ Poll Against.
P Absent, General Pair, "Present," Did not announce or answer Poll.
Democrats in this type; *Republicans in italics.*

SOURCE: *Congressional Quarterly Almanac,* vol. xx, 1964, p. 718.

APPENDIX V (continued)

	1.	10.
ALABAMA		
Hill	?	Y
Sparkman	Y	Y
ALASKA		
Bartlett	Y	N
Gruening	–	‡
ARIZONA		
Hayden	N	?
Goldwater	?	?
ARKANSAS		
Fulbright	Y	N
McClellan	Y	Y
CALIFORNIA		
Salinger	Y	Y
Kuchel	Y	Y
COLORADO		
Allott	N	Y
Dominick	N	Y
CONNECTICUT		
Dodd	N	Y
Ribicoff	Y	Y
DELAWARE		
Boggs	N	Y
Williams	N	Y

	1.	10.
FLORIDA		
Holland	N	Y
Smathers	?	‡
GEORGIA		
Russell	N	Y
Talmadge	N	Y
HAWAII		
Inouye	N	Y
Fong	N	Y
IDAHO		
Church	‡	‡
Jordan	N	Y
ILLINOIS		
Douglas	Y	N
Dirksen	X	‡
INDIANA		
Bayh	Y	‡
Hartke	?	‡
IOWA		
Hickenlooper	N	Y
Miller	N	Y
KANSAS		
Carlson	–	‡
Pearson	–	‡

	1.	10.
KENTUCKY		
Cooper	Y	Y
Morton	N	‡
LOUISIANA		
Ellender	X	√
Long	N	Y
MAINE		
Muskie	?	‡
Smith	N	Y
MARYLAND		
Brewster	–	‡
Beall	N	Y
MASSACHUSETTS		
Kennedy	√	X
Saltonstall	√	‡
MICHIGAN		
Hart	Y	N
McNamara	N	N
MINNESOTA		
Humphrey	?	‡
McCarthy	‡	‡
MISSISSIPPI		
Eastland	?	‡
Stennis	N	Y

	1.	10.
MISSOURI		
Long	Y	?
Symington	N	Y
MONTANA		
Mansfield	N	Y
Metcalf	Y	N
NEBRASKA		
Curtis	X	‡
Hruska	N	Y
NEVADA		
Bible	N	Y
Cannon	?	?
NEW HAMPSHIRE		
McIntyre	N	Y
Cotton	–	‡
NEW JERSEY		
Williams	‡	‡
Case	Y	Y
NEW MEXICO		
Anderson	N	N
Mechem	N	Y
NEW YORK		
Javits	Y	Y
Keating	Y	Y

APPENDIX V (continued)

NORTH CAROLINA	1.	10.
Ervin	N	Y
Jordan	N	Y
NORTH DAKOTA		
Burdick	–	‡
Young	N	Y
OHIO		
Lausche	N	Y
Young	–	
OKLAHOMA		
Edmondson	?	‡
Monroney	Y	N
OREGON		
Morse	N	Y
Neuberger	‡	‡

PENNSYLVANIA	1.	10.
Clark	Y	N
Scott	v	‡
RHODE ISLAND		
Pastore	N	‡
Pell	Y	N
SOUTH CAROLINA		
Johnston	N	Y
Thurmond	N	Y
SOUTH DAKOTA		
McGovern	Y	N
Mundt	N	Y
TENNESSEE		
Gore	Y	Y
Walters	N	N

TEXAS	1.	10.
Yarborough	N	Y
Tower	–	‡
UTAH		
Moss	N	Y
Bennett	N	Y
VERMONT		
Aiken	N	Y
Prouty	N	Y
VIRGINIA		
Byrd	–	Y
Robertson	N	‡
WASHINGTON		
Jackson	–	‡
Magnuson	N	Y

WEST VIRGINIA	1.	10.
Byrd	?	?
Randolph	Y	Y
WISCONSIN		
Nelson	Y	Y
Proxmire	N	Y
WYOMING		
McGee	Y	Y
Simpson	N	Y

APPENDIX VI

Questionnaire on Public Law 480 Issues: 1964

1. Did you favor continuation of Public Law 480 aid to communist nations?
        Yes........
        No........
        No position........

2. Did you support the establishment of an executive-legislative advisory committee?
        Yes........
        No........
        No position........

3. Did you support the period of extension and the amount of authorization for Public Law 480 as requested by the Administration?
        Yes........
        No........
        No position........

4. Did you envisage Public Law 480 as *essentially*:
        A program for the alleviation of domestic agricultural surpluses?
        ....
        A foreign aid program?........
        Or both?........

5. Did you favor Congressional supervision of Title I currency grants by means of the appropriations process?
        Yes........
        No........
        No position........

6. Did you favor withholding Public Law 480 aid to nations either waging aggression against nations having diplomatic relations with the United States or nations using United States funds of any type for purposes inimical to United States foreign policies?
        Yes........
        No........
        No position........

7. Did you favor the removal of the 25-percent limitation on Cooley loans?
        Yes........
        No........
        No position........

8. Did you favor prohibition of the use of United States-owned foreign currencies for the production of commodities in recipient countries if such commodities would compete with United States-produced commodities?

Yes........

No........

No position........

APPENDIX VII

Agricultural States

State[a]	Farm population 1964 — Rank	Farm population 1964 — Population (in thousands)	Farm population as percent of total 1964 — Rank	Farm population as percent of total 1964 — %	Total farm income 1963 — Rank	Total farm income 1963 — Income (in million dollars)	Farm income as percent of total 1963 — Rank	Farm income as percent of total 1963 — %	No. of farms 1964 — Rank	No. of farms 1964 — Total farms per state	Land in farms 1964 — Rank	Land in farms 1964 — Acres (in thousands)	Totals of rank coefficients	Rank of top 25 states
Alabama	14	342.58	15	10.06	21	300	13	5.0	13	101,000	27	16,100	103	19
Arizona	40	37.20	40	2.35	28	227	11	6.7	39	7,000	6	45,000	164	14
Arkansas	21	248.81	9	12.87	14	428	3	14.0	18	82,000	25	17,200	90	20
California	19	253.24	42	1.40	1	1,410	26	2.6	14	95,000	9	38,700	111	—
Colorado	31	94.86	28	4.82	32	178	23	3.0	28	33,000	8	41,000	150	—
Connecticut	44	21.05	46	0.08	40	57	34	0.67	38	7,700	45	990	247	—
Delaware	46	15.73	36	3.20	44	30	32	1.0	42	5,000	47	760	247	—
Florida	34	81.93	42	1.40	9	515	18	4.3	25	41,000	28	15,900	56	18
Georgia	12	345.50	21	8.00	17	367	20	4.0	15	91,000	18	20,000	103	—
Idaho	32	89.70	8	12.96	33	169	6	12.0	27	36,000	29	15,300	135	16
Illinois	9	396.35	34	3.78	4	828	25	2.7	7	144,000	15	30,300	94	15
Indiana	13	343.39	23	7.12	8	528	17	4.5	10	122,000	19	19,000	90	—
Iowa	4	438.16	4	15.89	3	944	3	14.0	3	170,000	12	34,600	29	1
Kansas	22	227.14	14	10.21	10	477	7	9.0	13	101,000	4	49,900	70	9
Kentucky	5	434.28	6	13.75	13	440	8	7.9	7	144,000	23	17,600	62	6
Louisiana	25	193.69	25	5.58	23	284	20	4.0	20	68,000	34	10,200	147	—
Maine	37	43.79	30	4.43	41	56	24	2.8	31	16,300	39	3,180	202	—
Maryland	33	82.65	39	2.41	37	85	33	0.9	30	23,600	38	3,550	210	—
Massachusetts	43	29.55	44	0.55	39	59	39	0.03	36	10,400	43	1,130	240	24
Michigan	15	314.01	32	3.90	19	339	29	1.6	12	105,000	30	14,300	127	4
Minnesota	8	407.40	11	11.40	6	623	9	7.6	6	146,000	14	32,400	54	5
Mississippi	6	405.14	3	17.60	11	448	3	14.0	11	114,000	20	18,600	54	7
Missouri	7	405.14	18	9.19	7	537	14	4.9	4	162,000	13	34,400	63	21
Montana	35	72.20	12	10.24	30	208	5	13.0	29	30,400	2	66,700	113	8
Nebraska	24	214.06	5	14.46	12	445	4	13.4	17	84,000	5	48,100	67	—
Nevada	47	7.82	41	1.92	45	18	30	1.4	43	2,200	36	8,800	242	—
New Hampshire	45	18.32	37	2.80	46	11	31	1.1	41	5,500	44	1,120	244	—

APPENDIX VII (continued)

State[a]	Farm population 1964 Population (in thousands)	Rank	Farm population as percent of total 1964 Rank	%	Total farm income 1963 Income (in million dollars)	Rank	Farm income as percent of total 1963 Rank	%	No. of farms 1964 Rank	Total farms per state	Land in farms 1964 Rank	Acres (in thousands)	Totals of rank coefficients	Rank of top 25 states
New Jersey	41.28	38	43	0.60	108	36	35	0.57	34	13,000	42	1,330	228	—
New Mexico	45.94	36	29	4.55	132	35	11	6.7	33	15,400	3	51,700	147	—
New York	251.95	20	45	0.14	366	18	36	0.5	19	72,000	31	13,500	169	—
N. Carolina	643.13	1	7	13.25	676	5	10	7.0	2	195,000	24	17,300	49	3
N. Dakota	141.11	27	1	21.87	289	22	1	22.2	23	50,500	7	42,100	81	10
Ohio	393.11	10	33	3.89	403	16	29	1.6	8	130,000	21	18,400	117	23
Oklahoma	216.34	23	19	8.78	242	27	20	4.0	16	88,000	10	37,300	115	22
Oregon	103.60	29	26	5.53	161	34	21	3.5	24	44,500	17	21,200	151	—
Pennsylvania	284.77	17	38	2.48	269	25	33	0.9	16	88,000	33	11,500	162	—
Rhode Island	3.46	48	47	0.48	6	47	37	0.27	44	1,200	48	125	271	—
S. Carolina	28.45	18	13	11.14	215	29	13	5.0	20	68,000	35	9,100	128	25
S. Dakota	143.36	26	2	20.05	280	24	2	20.0	21	53,500	6	45,000	81	11
Tennessee	466.20	3	10	12.30	322	20	15	4.8	5	154,000	26	16,200	100	17
Texas	538.45	2	27	5.18	1,115	2	12	5.2	1	210,000	1	154,000	45	2
Utah	34.32	41	35	3.72	51	42	27	2.4	32	15,800	31	13,500	208	—
Vermont	38.58	39	16	9.40	38	43	17	4.5	35	11,600	40	3,020	190	—
Virginia	313.80	16	22	7.20	179	31	28	2.0	16	88,000	32	13,100	145	—
Washington	120.70	28	31	4.04	256	26	22	3.3	22	52,000	22	18,200	151	—
W. Virginia	101.16	30	24	5.60	38	43	31	1.1	26	38,000	37	6,200	191	—
Wisconsin	382.27	11	17	9.30	405	15	19	4.2	9	127,000	16	21,600	87	12
Wyoming	29.90	42	20	8.70	77	38	7	9.0	37	9,600	11	35,800	87	13

[a] Alaska and Hawaii have not been included because of the lack of comparable data.

SOURCES: Compiled on the basis of data contained in: Bureau of the Census, *Statistical Abstract of the United States, 1965* (Washington, D.C., 1965), Table No. 11 (Population, Urban and Rural–States and Puerto Rico–1950 and 1960), p. 16; Table No. 457 (Personal Income–Major Sources by States–1963), pp. 332-333.

In estimating 1964 farm population data contained in Congressional Quarterly Publishers, *Congress and the Nation, 1945-1964* (Washington D.C., 1965), p. 381 was used.

Number of farms and land in farms are based on data contained in: Crop Reporting Board, *Number of Farms and Land in Farms, United States 1959-66, by States 1964-66* (Washington, D.C., January 12, 1966), pp. 1-3.

APPENDIX VIII

Public Law 480 States[a]

P.L. 480 rank No.	State	Coefficient of wheat and flour production*	Coefficient of cotton production*	Coefficient of dairy production*	Coefficient of feed grain production*	Coefficient of fats and oil production*	Coefficient of rice production*	Coefficient of production of other farm products*	Total coefficients of production*
1	Texas	33,188	64,821	355	7,848	22,011	19,818	2,465	150,506
2	Kansas	115,784	0	1,130	4,804	510	0	1,256	123,484
3	N. Dakota	85,886	0	710	5,381	677	0	550	93,204
4	California	4,387	28,129	6,960	3,058	6,632	16,171	18,827	84,164
5	Illinois	36,017	0	4,690	22,492	614	0	3,465	67,278
6	Oklahoma	51,889	4,573	3,550	115	1,499	0	1,499	63,025
7	Arkansas	7,561	25,022	527	29	7,372	18,661	778	59,950
8	Nebraska	40,461	0	861	9,738	479	0	1,969	53,463
9	Montana	48,542	0	108	173	8	0	884	49,715
10	Missouri	25,050	6,536	3,453	5,166	2,811	198	3,813	47,027
11	Minnesota	12,179	0	16,589	12,768	2,603	0	2,666	46,805
12	Mississippi	2,424	35,808	473	86	4,415	1,855	372	45,433
13	Indiana	27,821	0	1,700	10,373	2,822	0	2,186	44,902
14	Wisconsin	1,385	0	34,662	6,218	83	0	1,411	43,759
15	Ohio	23,318	0	8,553	6,723	1,760	0	2,690	43,044
16	Georgia	1,616	9,858	64	231	19,679	0	2,194	33,642
17	Michigan	21,529	0	3,561	3,967	323	0	1,930	31,310
18	N. Carolina	4,387	6,040	11	274	9,142	0	10,991	30,845
19	S. Dakota	21,702	0	1,538	4,847	364	0	1,620	30,071
20	Alabama	866	14,194	161	144	8,923	0	457	24,745
21	Tennessee	2,424	10,721	5,992	144	2,842	0	2,550	24,673
22	Iowa	1,443	0	7,165	5,107	4,987	0	3,511	22,213
23	Kentucky	2,828	129	7,832	188	146	0	5,836	16,959
24	S. Carolina	1,501	8,909	30	86	2,759	0	2,108	15,393
25	Wyoming	2,886	0	6	14	0	0	178	3,084

[a] Sources: Computed on the basis of data in U. S. Department of Agriculture, *Agricultural Statistics, 1965* (Washington, D. C.: Government Printing Office, 1966), and in charts developed by Food for Peace chartroom, Washington, D. C., as revised in 1964.

* The absolute production data for each state and each commodity has been weighted according to the relative importance of that commodity to total Public Law 480 agreements during the period 1955-1963. Totals of these coefficients appear in the last column which provides an index to the importance of Public Law 480 to a given state.

APPENDIX IX

Major Changes in Public Law 480 Made by the 1966 Extension and Amendment

1. Public Law 480 is extended for two years, through December 31, 1968.

2. Agreements for the sale of agricultural commodities for foreign currencies and dollar credit in each of these two years are authorized in an amount requiring appropriations not exceeding $1.9 billion plus the authority carried over from the preceding year (estimated at $1.7 billion as of December 31, 1966).

3. Title II Authority (donations) is $600 million per year, plus the carryover from the preceding year (estimated at $772 million as of December 31, 1966).

4. The short title of Public Law 480 is now "The Food for Peace Act of 1966."

5. The requirement that Food for Peace commodities be "surplus" has been removed.

6. The transition to dollar sales or sales for foreign currencies on terms as favorable to the United States as provided under Development Loan Fund loans must be accomplished within a five-year period (by December 31, 1971).

7. An increased emphasis has been placed upon "self-help" by recipient countries, and sales agreements must include descriptions of self-help measures.

8. Nations not having diplomatic relations with the United States, and nations selling or transporting to or from North Vietnam or Cuba are excluded from local currency or dollar credit sales. The President, however, may waive this prohibition in the case of certain specified nonstrategic agricultural materials and medical supplies sold or transported to or from Cuba.

9. Specific authority is granted for the use of foreign currencies for population control and farmer-to-farmer programs.

10. Five percent of the price on all sales must be paid in cash dollars whenever practicable.

11. Dollar sales credit agreements must specify the economic development to which the sales proceeds will be devoted.

12. Fourteen new members are added to the Advisory Committee: the Secretary of State, the Secretary of the Treasury, the second ranking majority and minority members of the House and Senate Agricultural committees, and the top two majority and minority members of the House and Senate foreign relations committees.

13.   Appropriations of up to $33 million per year are authorized for farmer-to-farmer technical assistance programs.

14.   The new law specifically states that section 620 (E) of the Foreign Assistance Act of 1961 applies to the assistance provided through sales under Public Law 480 (section 620 (E) prohibits assistance to countries expropriating property of United States citizens).

15.   The five-year limit on credit under dollar credit sales to Poland and other countries subject to the Battle Act is repealed.

16.   Title II (donation programs) is no longer restricted to CCC commodities.

17.   Up to 25 percent of foreign currencies received under future agreements must be convertible to cover American tourist expenses.

18.   Various provisions previously applicable to foreign currency sales are now extended to dollar credit sales, e.g., dollar limits on total agreements. Requirement that purchaser pay basic freight costs, restrictions on sales to the United Arab Republic and countries dealing with Cuba.

NOTES TO CHAPTER 1

1. The following analysis is presented largely in terms of social and political factors. The economic aspect of the farm problem is far more complex than supply and demand relationships. Regretfully, however, the esoteric nature of economic analyses of American agriculture defies meaningful summarization. The reader is referred to such works as the following for a more complete picture of the economics of agriculture: Geoffrey S. Shepard, *Farm Policy, New Directions* (Ames: Iowa State University Press, 1964); Edward Higbee, *Farms and Farmers in an Urban Age* (New York: Twentieth Century Fund, 1963); Dale E. Hathaway, *Problems of Progress in the Agricultural Economy* (Chicago: Scott, Foresman and Co., 1964); Dale E. Hathaway, *Government and Agriculture: Economic Policy in a Democratic Society* (New York: Macmillan, 1963); Willard W. Cochrane, *The City Man's Guide to the Farm Problem* (Minneapolis: University of Minnesota Press, 1965); Earl O. Heady, *et al, Roots of the Farm Problem* (Ames: Iowa State University Center for Agricultural and Economic Development, 1965); Willard W. Cochrane, *The Farm Problem: Myth or Reality?* (Minneapolis: University of Minnesota Press, 1958); Don Paarlberg, *American Farm Policy: A Case Study in Decentralized Decision Making* (New York: John Wiley and Sons, 1964); Murray Benedict, *Farm Policies of the United States, 1790-1950* (New York: Twentieth Century Fund, 1953).

2. United States Department of Agriculture, *Handbook of Agricultural Statistics* (Washington, D.C.: 1965), p. 25.

3. United States Law defines agricultural surpluses as commodities which are "in excess of domestic requirements, adequate carryover, and anticipated export for dollars, as determined by the Secretary of Agriculture." D. A. FitzGerald, *Operational and Administrative Problems of Food Aid* (Rome: United Nations World Food Program Studies #4, 1965), p. 2.

4. For a more extensive discussion, *cf.*: Hathaway, *Government and Agriculture, op. cit.*, Introduction, Chapters 1-3; *Farm Goals in Conflict* (Ames: Iowa State University Press, 1963); *Goals and Values in Agricultural Policy* (Ames: Iowa State University Center for Agricultural and Economic Adjustment, 1961).

5. Data from United States Department of Agriculture, "A Chronology of American Agriculture, 1790-1965," (chart) (Washington, D.C.: 1965).

6. Paarlberg, *op. cit.*, p. 108.

7. *Congress and the Nation: A Review of Government and Politics* (New York: Congressional Quarterly, Inc., 1965), p. 669; hereinafter cited as *Congress and the Nation*.

8. Paarlberg, *op. cit.*, p. 113.

9. The following discussion is largely based on: *Congress and the Nation*, pp. 673-676. Other relevant works include: Editors of the *Yale Law Journal*, "The Political Impasse in Farm Support Legislation," in Randall B. Ripley (ed.), *Public Policies and their Politics* (New York: W. W.

Norton, 1966), pp. 69-79; Charles M. Hardin, "Congressional Farm Politics and Economic Foreign Policy," *Annals* 331 (September 1960), pp. 98-103; Charles M. Hardin, "Farm Political Power and the U. S. Governmental Crisis," *Journal of Farm Economics* 40 (December 1958), pp. 1646-58; Thomas V. Gilpatrick, "Farm Price Support Legislation and the Midwest Farm Vote," *Midwest Journal of Political Science* 3 (November 1959), pp. 319-35; J. Roland Pennock, "Party and Constituency in Postwar Agricultural Price Support Legislation," *Journal of Politics* 18 (May 1956), pp. 167-211; Paarlberg, *op. cit.*, pp. 103-128; and George H. Mayer and Walter O. Forster, *The United States and the Twentieth Century* (Boston: Houghton Mifflin, 1958), *passim*.

10. Paarlberg, *op. cit.*, p. 123.

11. One of the most interesting works on agricultural interest groups is Wesley McCune, *Who's Behind Our Farm Policy?* (New York: Praeger, 1956), which is, unfortunately, now considerably out of date. See also: *Congress and the Nation*, pp. 676-677; Paarlberg, pp. 117-120; Lauren K. Soth, "Farm Policy, Foreign Policy, and Farm Opinion," and Ross B. Talbot, "Farm Organizations and the National Interest," in *Annals, op. cit.*, pp. 103-110 and 110-116, respectively; Hathaway, *Government and Agriculture, passim*.

12. Charles M. Hardin, "Farm Price Policy and the Farm Vote," *Journal of Farm Economics* 37 (November 1955), pp. 601-625; and Paarlberg, *op. cit.*, p. 114.

13. The following discussion is based on: The Yearly Summaries of Agricultural Legislation in *Congress and the Nation*, pp. 682-735; Shepard, *op. cit.*, Part 1; Hathaway, *Problems and Progress, op. cit., passim;* Benedict, *op. cit., passim;* Murray R. Benedict and Elizabeth K. Bauer, *Farm Surpluses: U.S. Burden or World Asset?* (Berkeley: University of California, 1960).

14. *Congress and the Nation*, pp. 665-666.

15. There are three distinct parity concepts: (1) the parity ratio, (2) parity price, and (3) parity income. By the parity ratio is meant a relationship between a selected group of prices paid to farmers and a selected group of prices paid by farmers. By parity price is meant a relationship between prices received for a single agricultural commodity in different time periods; a different parity price is computed for each commodity. Parity income relates the income of farmers to that of other producers in the economy. The parity concept appropriate for the present discussion is parity price, for commodity price support levels are based on parity price coefficients. Parity price coefficients are computed as index numbers with the base period specified as a time when prices for specific farm commodities were considered as "fair," usually 1910-14 or 1919-29 averages. Thus a parity price coefficient of 90, for example, indicates that prices for a given commodity are being supported at a rate of 10 percent less $(100 - 90 = 10)$ than the price of the base period.

16. *Cf. Congress and the Nation*, pp. 738-744 for a seminal discussion of surplus disposal programs.

17. CCC holdings account for only about 90 percent of the agricultural carryover of the United States—the remainder is held in private stocks. For information concerning this private carryover, see USDA, *Agricultural Statistics, 1965* (Washington, D.C.: Government Printing Office, 1966), *passim* and USDA, *Handbook of Agricultural Statistics, passim*.

NOTES TO CHAPTER 2

1. While there is agreement on the following classification among most authorities, the terminology and illustrative data are taken from D. A. FitzGerald, "Foreign Assistance Programs," in the United States Department of Agriculture, *The Yearbook of Agriculture, 1964*, 88th Congress, 2nd session, House Document #279 (Washington, D.C.: 1964), pp. 495-499. For a more detailed discussion, the reader is referred to: Edward S. Mason, *Foreign Aid and Foreign Policy* (New York: Harper and Row, 1964); *Congress and the Nation: A Review of Government and Politics* (New York: Congressional Quarterly, Inc., 1965), pp. 160-185; James A. Robinson, *Congress and Foreign Policy Making* (Homewood: Dorsey Press, 1962); John D. Montgomery, *The Politics of Foreign Aid: American Experience in Southeast Asia* (New York: Praeger, 1962); Peter B. Kenen, *Giant Among Nations: Problems in United States Foreign Economic Policy* (Chicago: Rand McNally Company, 1960); and H. Bradford Westerfield, *Foreign Policy and Party Politics* (New Haven: Yale University Press, 1955).

2. Hollis B. Chenery, "Objectives and Criteria for Foreign Assistance," in R. A. Goldwin, ed., *Why Foreign Aid?* (Chicago: Rand McNally, 1963), p. 33.

3. Food aid is defined by D. A. FitzGerald, *Operational and Administrative Problems of Food Aid* (Rome: United Nations World Food Program Studies #4, 1965), p. 1, in the following manner:

. . . Food aid is defined to include (A) agricultural commodities, usually but not invariably in surplus, furnished as "aid" to receiving countries and (B) monetary resources that may be used only for (1) the purchase, processing, packaging, and transportation of such commodities and (2) costs of administration. It does not include similar commodities purchased by the receiving countries, on generally prevailing commercial terms, with their own foreign exchange resources or with foreign aid that is not tied to the purchase of these particular commodities. In addition to edible commodities, the bilateral food aid program of the United States, but so far not the multilateral program, includes cotton, tobacco, inedible oils, and seeds.

Under this definition, the large quantities of agricultural commodities provided in the immediate postwar years by the United Nations Relief and Rehabilitation Administration, as part of the European Recovery Program, would not be considered food aid since the "aid" used to purchase these agricultural commodities could have been used to procure other commodities if the latter had a higher priority; that is, the aid was not tied to the purchase of specific agricultural commodities.

The *raison d'etre* for food aid is that certain countries, notably the

United States, can make more total resources available to other, usually developing, countries if a part thereof is in the form of surplus agricultural commodities. Production of certain agricultural products, primarily as the result of domestic agricultural policies, exceeds the effective market demand, therefore, at politically acceptable prices, and providing all or part of these surpluses to developing countries is a more attractive and constructive (and frequently less expensive) alternative than storing them indefinitely or destroying them.

4. The following discussion is based on two excellent works: V. M. Dandekar, *The Demand for Food, and Conditions Governing Food Aid During Development* (Rome: United Nations World Food Program Studies #1, 1965), pp. 1-20; and United States Department of Agriculture, Economic Research Service, Foreign Regional Analysis Division, *The World Food Budget, 1970* (Washington, D.C.: Foreign Agricultural Economic Report #19, October 1964), pp. 1-60. Additional references include the following: George Borgstrom, *The Hungry Planet* (New York: Macmillan, 1965); L. H. Lebret, *The Last Revolution* (New York: Sheed and Ward, 1965); Jonathan Garst, *No Need for Hunger* (New York: Random House, 1963); Michel Cepede, Francois Houtart, and Linus Grond, *Population and Food* (New York: Sheed and Ward, 1964); Graduate students at the Harvard Business School, *The Protein Paradox* (Boston: Management Reports, 1964); I. W. Moomaw, *Crusade Against Hunger* (New York: Harper and Row, 1966).

5. The FAO has estimated in *Agricultural Commodities: Projections for 1970* (Rome: Special Supplement to FAO Commodity Review, 1962) that in terms of national calorie production and calorie requirements, only nations in the Far East have and will have serious deficits; for a discussion of the serious limitations of this estimate, C. F. Dandekar, *The Demand for Food*, pp. 1-20.

6. USDA, *World Food Budget*, *op. cit.*, p. 30.

7. Dandekar, *The Demand for Food*, *op. cit.*, p. 19.

8. The following discussion is based on FitzGerald, *Operational and Administrative Problems*, *op. cit.*, pp. 2-5.

9. The following treatment of the origins of Public Law 480 is based on: David S. McClellan and Donald Clare, *Public Law 480: The Metamorphosis of a Law* (New York: McGraw-Hill; Eagleton Institute Cases in Practical Politics, 1965), pp. 2-4; and Elmer L. Menzie and Robert G. Crouch, *Political Interests in Agricultural Export Surplus Disposal Through Public Law 480* (Tucson: University of Arizona Experiment Station, Technical Bulletin #161, September 1964), pp. 9-10. Since these two works complement one another, the author has taken the liberty of presenting a synthesis which has been supplemented by *Congressional Quarterly Almanac, 1953 and 1954*, Vols. IX and X, pp. 114 and 120-124, respectively.

10. McClellan and Clare, *op. cit.*, p. 2.

11. Menzie and Crouch, *op. cit.*, p. 9.

12. *Congressional Quarterly Almanac*, 1954, Vol. X, p. 121.

13. The following is based on *ibid.*, p. 123.

14. *Ibid.*, p. 124.

15. For a complete record of Public Law 480 extensions and amendments, *cf. Agricultural Trade Development and Assistance Act of 1954 and Amendments*, as compiled by Gilman G. Udell, Superintendent, Documents Room, House of Representatives (Washington, D.C.: Government Printing Office, 1962).

16. This section largely summarizes McClellan and Clare, *op. cit.*, pp. 26-32 and George S. McGovern, *War Against Want: America's Food for Peace Program* (New York: Walker and Company, 1964), pp. vii-xvi. Further information of interest is contained in U.S. Congress, Senate, Hubert H. Humphrey, *Food and Fiber as a Force for Freedom*: A Report, 85th Congress, 2nd session (Washington, D.C.: Government Printing Office, April, 1958); U.S. Congress, Senate, Hubert H. Humphrey, *Economic Development in Underdeveloped Areas Through the Use of Agricultural Surpluses*, 87th Congress, 1st session, Calendar No. 262, Report No. 290 to accompany S. 1720 (Washington, D.C.: Government Printing Office, May 26, 1961); and Winthrop Griffith, *Humphrey: A Candid Biography* (New York: William Morrow and Co., 1965), pp. 272-274.

17. McGovern, *ibid.*, pp. xi-xii.

18. *Ibid.*, p. xii. A synopsis of the Executive Orders and Memoranda related to the establishment of the Food for Peace program is contained in U.S. Congress, House of Representatives, Committee on Appropriations, Subcommittee on Agriculture, *Appropriations for the Department of Agriculture and Related Agencies for 1962: Hearings on H.R. 7444*, part 2, 87th Congress, 1st session (Washington, D.C.: Government Printing Office, May, 1961), pp. 843ff.

19. The difference between the new emphasis and that of the prior Food for Peace program, as established by President Eisenhower, emerges clearly in the writings of the two past directors of the program. Paarlberg in his *American Farm Policy* (New York: John Wiley and Sons, 1964), pp. 288-295, stresses the domestic benefits resultant from Public Law 480; McGovern, *op. cit.*, on the other hand, discusses Public Law 480 completely in the context of foreign assistance.

20. The organization, structure, and operation of Food for Peace is a complex subject matter which precludes detailed analysis. Since this study pertains to the executive-legislative interactions of Food for Peace during the 1964 extension, the following discussion will treat only the appropriate organizational characteristics of the Food for Peace program.

21. The White House Office of Food for Peace was transferred to the State Department in 1966, as will be discussed in detail in Chapter 7.

22. *Agricultural Trade Development and Assistance Act of 1954 and Amendments, op. cit., passim.*

23. Except where otherwise noted, the following discussion is largely based on: "Program Assistance; Public Law 480, Title I, Sales of Surplus Agricultural Commodities for Foreign Currencies," *Agency for International*

Development Manual, Order #1142-1, Trans. letter #10.8, effective date September 30, 1963, pp. 1-2.

24. The following synopsis of Executive Order 10900 is taken from: *ibid., passim,* and "Program Assistance: Public Law 480, General," *AID Manual,* Order #1141.1, Trans. letter #10.8, effective date September 30, 1963, pp. 1-2.

25. "Public Law 480, General," *ibid.,* p. 1.

26. *Ibid.*

27. Office of the White House, Director of Food for Peace, *The Annual Report on Activities Carried Out Under Public Law 480, 83rd Congress as Amended, During the Period January 1 through December 31, 1964,* House Document #130-89/1 (Washington, D.C.: Government Printing Office, March 24, 1965), p. 17; hereafter cited as "Annual Report, 1964."

28. *Cf., Agricultural Trade Development and Assistance Act of 1954 and Amendments, op. cit.,* p. 4.

29. Much of the following is based on: "Program Assistance: Public Law 480, Grants of Surplus Agricultural Commodities (Section 202), *AID Manual,* Order #1143.1, Trans. letter #10.9, effective date September 30, 1963, pp. 1-11.

30. *Ibid.,* pp. 1-2.

31. *Ibid.,* p. 2.

32. *Ibid.*

33. *Ibid.*

34. From *Public Law 480 Handbook,* Part II, Detailed Operations and Procedures Under Public Law Title II—Use of Agricultural Commodities for Emergency Assistance (Section 201) and Economic Development (Section 202) Programs, pp. 3-4.

35. See *Agricultural Trade Development and Assistance Act of 1954 and Amendments, op. cit.,* pp. 4-6, 20-22.

36. For description of these non-Food for Peace Title III operations, see: Foreign Agricultural Service, *Department of Agriculture, Barter Program (Title III Public Law 480),* dittoed memorandum dated April 15, 1964; and *Annual Report, 1964, op. cit.,* pp. 81, 87-91, 139-144.

37. Organizations authorized for participation in Title III foreign donation programs in 1964 were: CARE, Catholic Relief Service, Church World Service, UNICEF, Lutheran World Relief, American Jewish Joint Distribution Committee, American Mission to Greeks, American National Red Cross, American Relief for Poland, Foreign Service Committee-Assemblies of God, Hadassah, Mennonite Central Committee, People to People Health Foundation, Seventh-Day Adventist Welfare Service, United Nations Relief and Works Agency, Volunteer Border Relief, and the National Association of Evangelicals.

38. Except as otherwise noted, the following is based on: "Public Law 480, Title III, Introduction," *AID Manual,* Order #1556.1, Trans. letter

#18.5, effective date August 11, 1964, pp. 1-4; and "Public Law 480, Title III, Program Responsibility," *AID Manual*, Order #1557.1, Trans. letter #18.6, effective date August 11, 1964, pp. 1-5.

39. "Chapter XV—Donation of Food Commodities for Use in the Assistance of Needy Persons and in Non-Profit School Lunch Programs Outside the United States of America, From the Manual of Foreign Agricultural Service, Department of Agriculture, in *AID Manual*, Order #1158.1, Trans. letter #817, Attachment A, effective date August 11, 1964, p. A2.

40. *Cf. Agricultural Trade Development and Assistance Act of 1954 and Amendments, op. cit.*, pp. 22-23, 30-31.

41. Except where otherwise noted, the following is based on: "Program Assistance: Public Law 480, Title IV, Sales of Surplus Agricultural Commodities for Dollars," *AID Manual*, Order #1145.1, Trans. letter #10.10, effective date September 30, 1963, pp. 1-2.

42. From Senator Ellender's remarks about the program on the floor of the Senate as contained in the *Congressional Record* [daily edition], August 19, 1964, p. 19777.

43. *Annual Report, op. cit.*, pp. 23-24.

44. The following is calculated from data contained in *ibid.*, p. 117.

NOTES TO CHAPTER 3

1. For a detailed examination of Congressional attitudes toward Public Law 480, 1954-1962, see Elmer L. Menzie and Robert G. Crouch, *Political Interests in Agricultural Export Surplus Disposal Through Public Law 480* (Tucson: Arizona Agricultural Experiment Station, Technical Bulletin 161, September, 1964). The annual *Congressional Quarterly Almanac, 1954-1964*, also contains excellent material. The following discussion draws heavily from these sources.

2. *Congressional Quarterly Almanac*, 1957, Vol. XIII, p. 641.

3. *Ibid.*, p. 642, as quoted from Senate Report 188, March 26, 1957.

4. As quoted in Menzie and Crouch, *op. cit.*, p. 11.

5. *Congressional Quarterly Almanac*, Vol. XV, p. 230.

6. *Ibid.*, p. 234.

7. *Ibid.*, p. 234.

8. *Ibid.*, p. 235.

9. *Ibid.*, p. 236.

10. *Congressional Quarterly Almanac*, 1961, Vol. XVII, p. 107.

11. See the comments of Assistant Secretary for Economic Affairs, Edward M. Martin, in the House hearings on May 23, 1961. *Congressional Quarterly Almanac*, 1961, Vol. XVII, p. 109. This is not to imply, however, that the program was entirely free from Congressional criticism in 1961: see the "Statement on Policy" endorsed by both House and Senate confer-

ees as contained in *Congressional Record* [daily edition], August 3, 1961, pp. 14563-14564.

12. The Congressional image of Public Law 480 during 1963 will be discussed in the following chapter as a prelude to the formulation of the 1964 Executive request.

13. These two systems of decision making during extension periods should not be confused with the Public Law 480 or Food for Peace operations as one and the same system. The description of the Executive and Congressional systems follows the model presented by David Easton, "An Approach to the Analysis of Political Systems," *World Politics*, IX (April, 1957), pp. 383-400.

NOTES TO CHAPTER 4

1. As contained in United States Congress, Senate Committee on Agriculture and Forestry, *Hearings: Extension and Amendment of Public Law 480, 83rd Congress*, 88th Congress, 2d Session, August 12, 1964, p. 7. These hearings will hereafter be cited as "Senate Hearings, 1964."

2. The participants in this conference included representatives of the White House Food for Peace Office, The Department of Agriculture, AID, the National Academy of Sciences, and interest groups (primarily farm groups). Several private citizens who did not represent organizations also participated in the conference.

3. See *Congressional Quarterly*, XXII, #6, February 7, 1964, p. 283.

4. *Food for Peace*, #3, May 1963, p. 4.

5. *Congressional Record* [daily edition], August 19, 1964, p. 19789.

6. United States Congress, Senate Committee on Appropriations, Senator Gale W. McGee, *Personnel Administration and Operations of Agency for International Development* (Washington, D.C.: Government Printing Office, November 29, 1963), pp. 39-40; hereafter cited as the "McGee Report."

7. *Ibid.*

8. *Senate Hearings, op. cit.*, 1964, pp. 27-28.

9. United States Congress, House Committee on Agriculture, Subcommittee on Foreign Agricultural Operations, *Hearings: Extension of Public Law 480—Title I and II*, 88th Congress, 2d Session, February 18, 19, 20 and 28, 1964, p. 158; hereafter cited as "House Hearings, 1964."

10. A summary of the contents of the four documents is available in *Food for Peace*, #10 (January 1964), pp. 4-6.

11. For details on the Executive presentation to Congress, see Chapter 5.

12. Ironically, it was Senator Humphrey who saw the handwriting on the wall and pleaded the case as early as 1954 for legislation which would have bypassed the major contradiction between domestic and foreign policy interests.

13. *House Hearings, op. cit.*, 1964, p. 158.

NOTES TO CHAPTER 5

1. *House Hearings, 1964, op. cit.*, pp. 12-16.

2. *Ibid.*, p. 13.

3. *Ibid.*, p. 22.

4. *Ibid.*, p. 24.

5. *Ibid.*, p. 43.

6. *Ibid.*, p. 17.

7. *Ibid.*, p. 138.

8. *Ibid.*, p. 140.

9. *Ibid.*, pp. 144-145.

10. *Ibid.*, p. 167.

11. *Ibid.*, p. 145.

12. *Ibid.*, pp. 27-28; 65; 84ff.

13. For a complete synopsis of the provisions of the bill, see Appendix III.

14. See items #26 and #27 of Appendix III.

15. Mr. Findley from the Committee on Agriculture, *Report: Additional Views*, 88th Congress, 2d Session, House of Representatives, Report #1767, Part 2, pp. 1-3.

16. See *Senate Hearings, 1964, op. cit.*, p. 31.

17. For a complete synopsis of the provisions of the Senate bill as introduced, see Appendix III.

18. *Senate Hearings, 1964, op. cit.*, p. 23.

19. *Ibid.*, pp. 23-24.

20. *Ibid.*, p. 26.

21. *Ibid.*, p. 29.

22. *Ibid.*, p. 79.

23. For a complete synopsis of the provisions of this bill, see Appendix III.

24. *Congressional Record* [daily edition], August 17, p. 19326.

25. *Congressional Record* [daily edition], September 2, p. 20770.

26. *Ibid.*, pp. 20770-20779.

27. *Congressional Record* [daily edition], September 3, p. 20229.

28. *Ibid.*, pp. 20933-20934.

29. *Congressional Record* [daily edition], August 19, p. 19788.

30. Mr. Ellender from the Committee on Agriculture and Forestry, *Report: Extension and Amendment of Public Law 480*, 88th Congress, 2d Session, Report #1467, August 18, 1964, p. 28.

31. *Congressional Quarterly*, XXII, #34, August 21, 1964, p. 1915.

32. *Congressional Record* [daily edition], August 19, pp. 19784-19785.

33. *Ibid.*, pp. 19780-19784.

34. *Congressional Record* [daily edition], September 23, p. 21876.

35. While this conclusion is the result of independent research, it must be pointed out that the *Congressional Quarterly Almanac*, 1964, Vol. XX, pp. 130-132, in an excellent summary, reaches essentially the same conclusion. In some instances, the language of the *Congressional Quarterly Almanac* summary, because of its lucidity, has been incorporated into the following discussion.

36. For a synopsis of the differences between the House and Senate bills, as passed, see Appendix III.

37. *Congressional Record* [daily edition], September 22, p. 21758.

38. *Ibid.*, p. 21926.

39. *Ibid.*, p. 21927.

40. *Congressional Record* [daily edition], September 24, p. 22062.

41. *Ibid.*, pp. 33-35.

42. *Congressional Record* [daily edition], September 23, p. 21877.

NOTES TO CHAPTER 6

1. Interviews with eight key members of the House Committee on Agriculture and the Subcommittee on Foreign Agricultural Operations, including staff members, were conducted by the author during the spring of 1965.

2. The liberal-conservative concept used herein is based upon the *Congressional Quarterly Almanac*, which gives the percentage of times a member supported or opposed the stand of Republicans and Southern Democrats when a majority of Republicans, joined by a majority of Southern Democrats, opposed the majority of Northern Democrats. See *ibid.*, Vol. XX, 1964, pp. 752-754. The average conservative support score of the seven respondents in the House subcommittee was 57.1 percent conservative and 32.6 percent liberal.

3. It is interesting to note that two Republicans, who were opposed to the measure in the subcommittee, failed to vote in the role call on this issue on the floor of the House. Furthermore, there were three Democrats who supported and one Republican who opposed such aid. None of these congressmen answered the questionnaire.

4. The average conservative support score of the eleven respondents in the Senate committee was 55.2 percent conservative and 33.2 percent liberal.

5. The average conservative support score of the nine respondents in the conference committee was 73.4 percent conservative and 16.3 percent liberal.

6. It should be pointed out that, in a roll-call vote on the floor of the Senate dealing with this issue, three Republicans opposed the continuation of such aid, while one Democrat failed to vote.

7. See Appendices IV and V.

8. Those opposed were: Congressmen Passman (D-Louisiana), Curtis (R-Missouri), Dorn (D-South Carolina), Quillen (R-Tennessee), Forman (R-Texas), and Stinson (R-Washington). The average conservative-support score of this group was 83.2 percent conservative and 6.5 percent liberal.

9. Senators voting against the bill were: Bartlett (D-Alaska), Fulbright (D-Arkansas), Douglas (D-Illinois), Hart (D-Michigan), McNamara (D-Michigan), Metcalf (D-Montana), Anderson (D-New Mexico), Monroney (D-Oklahoma), Clark (D-Pennsylvania), Pell (D-Rhode Island), and McGovern (D-South Dakota). The average conservative support score of this group was 14.1 percent conservative and 74.3 percent liberal.

10. Weights were assigned to interviewee's responses according to the following system: A response supporting the Administration was a plus ($+$); a response opposing the Administration was a minus ($-$); and a response expressing no preference was a plus-minus($\pm$). See Appendix VI for the text of the questionnaire.

11. Our desire to include the variable of urban-rural division was frustrated by the unavailability of 1964 data. As Paul C. Glick, Acting Chief, Population Division, Bureau of the Census explained in his May 5, 1966 letter: "The Census Bureau has made no estimates of the urban and rural population for States, nor do we know of any source for these data."

12. The rank order position of attendance at committee hearings was included in the conference committee (in spite of its tenuous position there) for the sake of comparability in calculations of X^2 significance.

13. See our discussion on this problem in Chapter 6, p. 00.

NOTES TO CHAPTER 7

1. As quoted in the *Congressional Quarterly Almanac,* Vol. XX, 1964, p. 132.

2. One interpretation of the intent of Public Law 480 was offered by Congressman Charles B. Hoeven (R-Iowa): "I voluntarily retired from Congress on January 1, 1965 after 32 years of continuous service. I helped write the original P.L. 480 and took an active part in considering amendments to the legislation for many years. It was originally intended that P.L. 480 should be for the orderly disposal of surplus agricultural commodities but it has now become only an adjunct to the foreign aid programs, much to my regret." Personal letter to the author from former Congressman Hoeven, dated January 8, 1966.

3. *Foreign Affairs Manual Circular,* No. 36B, October 29, 1965. Reuter resigned from his post as Special Assistant to the Secretary of State for Food for Peace, on January 15, 1967.

4. United States Congress, House of Representatives, Committee on Agriculture, Parts 1, 2 and 3, Serial W. 89th Congress, 2nd Session. Because of the interest expressed by many members of the Committee on Agriculture, Chairman Cooley used his discretion to assign the hearings to the full committee instead of the sub-committee.

5. U. S. Congress, Senate, Committee on Agriculture and Forestry, Mr. Ellender, *A Report: Food for Peace Act of 1966*, 89th Congress, 2nd session, Report No. 1527 (August 25, 1966), p. 10.

6. For a detailed summary of the provisions of Public Law 89-638, see Appendix IX.

7. Since this study did not examine the entire House committee, our extrapolation of past Congressional attitudes to the present and future food aid legislation will be restricted to the role of the Southern Democrats in the Senate committee.

8. *Congressional Record* [daily edition], June 17, 1965, p. 5.

9. *Ibid.*, p. 1.

10. "Senator Allen J. Ellender Reports from Congress." Text of Radio Address Recorded by Louisiana's Senior Senator, Broadcast over Radio Station WWL, New Orleans, Louisiana, Saturday, July 30, 1966, p. 4.

11. *Congressional Record* [daily edition], August 29, 1966.

12. *Ibid.*, p. 20218.

NOTE TO APPENDIX II

1. Reproduced from Representative Cooley's *Report on the Extension and Amendment of Public Law 480*, House of Representatives, 88th Congress, 2d Session, Report No. 1767, August 11, 1964, pp. 36-38. An identical letter was sent to Carl Hayden, President Pro Tempore of the Senate, on the same date.

NOTES TO APPENDIX III

1. As contained in a letter from Secretary Freeman to both the President Pro Tempore of the Senate, Hon. Carl Hayden, and John W. McCormack, Speaker of the House of Representatives, dated February 18, 1964, which was accompanied by a draft of a proposed bill. A reproduction of this letter is to be found in: U.S. Congress, Senate Committee on Agriculture and Forestry, Mr. Ellender, "Report on Extension and Amendment of Public Law 480 (to accompany S. 2687)," 88th Congress, 2d Session, Report #1467, Calendar #1402, pp. 31-33. This letter will be referred to as the "Executive Request."

2. S. 2687 "A Bill to Extend the Agricultural Trade Development Act, and for Other Purposes," 88th Congress, 2d Session; hereafter cited as "S. 2687, as introduced."

3. As contained in Senate Report #1467, Calendar #1402, *op. cit.*, pp. 1-2, 44-52; hereafter cited as "S. 2687, as reported."

4. As contained in *Congressional Record*, September 3, 1964, pp. 20935-20936 among other places; hereafter cited as "S. 2687, as passed on floor."

5. H.R. 12298, "A Bill to Extend the Agricultural Trade Development and Assistance Act of 1954, and for Other Purposes," 88th Congress, 2d

Session, Union Calendar #782; hereafter cited as "H.R. 12298, as introduced."

6. As contained in U.S. Congress, House of Representatives, Committee on Agriculture, Mr. Cooley, "Report to Accompany H. R. 12298: Extension and Amendment of Public Law 480," 88th Congress, 2d Session, Report #1767, pp. 1-3, 34-47; hereafter cited as "H.R. 12298, as reported."

7. As contained in *Congressional Record,* September 3, 1964, p. 20936 among other places; hereafter cited as "H.R. 12298, as passed on floor."

8. As provided by Public Law 88-638, 78 Stat. 1035 as contained in: Foreign Agricultural Service, USDA, Public Law 480, 83d Congress, Chapter 469, 2d Session, S. 2495; as amended through October 31, 1964 (Washington, D.C.: Government Printing Office), *passim;* hereafter cited as "Public Law 88-638."

9. The following summary of PL 88-638 provisions is based on that contained in *Annual Report, 1964,* pp. 96-97.

10. Public Law 88-638 amending Secs. 104 and 109 of Public Law 480.

11. H.R. 12298, as introduced, parag. 1 and 7 of Section 1.

12. H.R. 12298, as reported, parag. 1 and 7 of Section 1.

13. H.R. 12298, as passed on the floor, parag. 1 and 7 of Section 1.

14. S. 2687, as introduced, parag. 10 of Section 1.

15. Executive Request, parag. 1.

16. S. 2687, as reported, parag. 12 of Section 1.

17. S. 2687, as passed on the floor, parag. 12 of Section 1.

18. *Cf.* Executive Request, parag. 6; S. 2687, as introduced, parag. 9 of Section 1; S. 2687, as reported, parag. 12 of Section 1; S. 2687, as passed on the floor, parag. 12 of Section 1; H.R. 12298, as introduced, parag. 8 of Section 1; H.R. 12298, as reported, parag. 8 of Section 1; and H.R. 12298, as passed on the floor, parag. 7 of Section 1; and Public Law 88-638 amending Section 203 of Public Law 480.

19. Public Law 88-638 amending Section 103 (b) of Public Law 480.

20. H.R. 12298, as introduced, parag. 1 of Section 1; H.R. 12298, as reported, parag. 1 of Section 1; H.R. 12298, as passed on the floor, parag. 1 of Section 1.

21. Executive Request, parag. 6.

22. S. 2687, as introduced, parag. 3 of Section 1.

23. S. 2687, as reported, parag. 5 of Section 1.

24. S. 2687, as passed, parag. 5 of Section 1.

25. Public Law 88-638 amending Section 203 of Public Law 480.

26. H. R. 12298, as introduced, parag. 8 of Section 1; H.R. 12298, as reported, parag. 8 of Section 1; H.R. 12298, as passed on the floor, parag. 8 of Section 1.

27. Executive Request, parag. 6.

28. S. 2687, as introduced, parag. 9 of Section 1.

29. S. 2687, as reported, parag. 11 of Section 1.

30. S. 2687, as passed on the floor, parag. 11 of Section 1.

31. Public Law 88-638 amending Section 107 of Public Law 480.

32. H.R. 12298, as passed on the floor, parag. 5 of Section 1.

33. Public Law 88-638 amending Section 107 of Public Law 480.

34. H.R. 12298, as passed on the floor, parag. 11 of Section 1.

35. Public Law 88-638 amending Section 102 of Public Law 480.

36. *Annual Report, 1964,* p. 96.

37. S. 2687, as introduced, parag. 2 of Section 1.

38. S. 2687, as reported, parag. 3 of Section 1.

39. S. 2687, as passed on the floor, parag. 3 of Section 1.

40. Public Law 88-638 amending Section 101 (f) of Public Law 480.

41. S. 2687, as introduced, parag. 8 and 11 of Section 1.

42. H.R. 12298, as introduced, parag. 11 of Section 1.

43. S. 2687, as reported, parag. 1 of Section 1.

44. H.R. 12298, as reported, parag. 10 of Section 1; H.R. 12298, as passed on the floor, parag. 10 of Section 1; S. 2687, as passed on the floor, parag. 1 of Section 1.

45. Public Law 88-638 amending Section 104 of Public Law 480.

46. H.R. 12298, as introduced, parag. 4 of Section 1.

47. H.R. 12298, as reported, parag. 4 of Section 1.

48. H.R. 12298, as passed, contains no provision.

49. Public Law 88-638 amending Section 104 of Public Law 480.

50. *Ibid.*

51. S. 2687, as reported, parag. 8 of Section 1.

52. H.R. 12298, as introduced, parag. 5 of Section 1.

53. S. 2687, as passed, parag. 8 of Section 1; H.R. 12298, as reported, parag. 5 of Section 1; H.R. 12298, as passed on the floor, parag. 4 of Section 1.

54. Public Law 88-638 amending Section 101 (g) of Public Law 480.

55. S. 2687, as introduced, parag. 1 of Section 1.

56. S. 2687, as reported, parag. 2 and 9 of Section 1.

57. S. 2687, as passed on the floor, parag. 2 and 9 of Section 1.

58. Public Law 88-638 amending Section 403 of Public Law 480.

59. S. 2687, as introduced, parag. 12 of Section 1.

60. S. 2687, as reported, parag. 13 of Section 1.

61. S. 2687, as passed on the floor, parag. 14 of Section 1.

62. Public Law 88-638 amending Section 104 of Public Law 480.

63. S. 2687, as introduced, parag. 7 of Section 1.

64. S. 2687, as reported, parag. 9 of Section 1; and S. 2687, as passed on the floor, parag. 7 of Section 1.

65. H.R. 12298, as reported, parag. 9 of Section 1.

66. H.R. 12298, as introduced, parag. 10 of Section 1; H.R. 12298, as passed on the floor, parag. 9 of Section 1.

67. Executive Request, parag. 3.

68. S. 2687, as introduced, parag. 5 of Section 1; S. 2687, as reported, parag. 7 of Section 1; S. 2687, as passed on the floor, parag. 7 of Section 1; H.R. 12298, as introduced, parag. 3 of Section 1; H.R. 12298, as reported, parag. 3 of Section 3.

69. H.R. 12298, as passed on the floor, contains no such provision.

70. Public Law 88-638 adding Section 104 (t) to Public Law 480.

71. H.R. 12298, as introduced, Section 2.

72. H.R. 12298, as reported, Section 2; H.R. 12298, as passed on the floor, Section 2; S. 2687, as reported, Section 2; S. 2687, as passed, Section 2.

73. Public Law 88-638 amending Section 104 (c) of Public Law 480.

74. Executive Request, parag. 2; S. 2687, as introduced, parag. 4 of Section 1; S. 2687, as reported, parag. 6 of Section 1; S. 2687, as passed on the floor, parag. 6 of Section 1; H.R. 12298, as introduced, parag. 2 of Section 1; H.R. 12298, as reported, parag. 2 of Section 1; H.R. 12298, as passed on the floor, parag. 2 of Section 1.

75. Executive Request, parag. 6; S. 2687, as introduced, parag. 9 of Section 1; S. 2687, as reported, parag. 11 of Section 1; S. 2687, as passed on the floor, parag. 11 of Section 1; H.R. 12298, as introduced, parag. 8 of Section 1; H.R. 12298, as reported, parag. 8 of Section 1; H.R. 12298, as passed on the floor, parag. 8 of Section 1; Public Law 88-638 amending Section 203 of Public Law 480.

76. Public Law 88-638 amending Section 304 (a) of Public Law 480.

77. S. 2687, as passed, parag. 13 of Section 1.

78. H.R. 12298, as passed, parag. 12 of Section 1.

79. Executive Request, parag. 5.

80. S. 2687, as introduced, parag. 11 of Section 1.

81. S. 2687, as reported, parag. 10 of Section 1; S. 2687, as passed, parag. 10 of Section 1; H.R. 12298, as introduced, parag. 7 of Section 7; H.R. 12298, as reported, parag. 7 of Section 1; H.R. 12298, as passed, parag. 6 of Section 1.

82. Public Law 88-683 amending Section 302 (416) of Public Law 480.

83. H.R. 12298, as introduced, Section 3; H.R. 12298, as reported, Section 3; H.R. 12298, as passed on the floor, Section 3.

84. One additional provision was passed which concerned the eligibility of extra long staple cotton, cf. S. 2687, as passed, Section 3. Since this provision does not bear on the Food for Peace program it will not be discussed here.

85. Public Law 88-638 amending Section 103 of Public Law 480.
86. S. 2687, as reported, parag. 4 of Section 1.
87. S. 2687, as passed on the floor, parag. 4 of Section 1.
88. Executive Request, parag. 4.
89. S. 2687, as introduced, parag. 6 of Section 1.
90. Executive Request, parag. 4.
91. S. 2687, as introduced, parag. 6 of Section 1.
92. H.R. 12298, as introduced, parag. 4 of Section 1.
93 H.R. 12298, as reported, parag. 4 of Section 1.
94. H.R. 12298, as introduced, parag. 4 of Section 1.
95. H.R. 12298, as passed, parag. 3 of Section 1.

Index

Abernathy, Thomas G., 41
Adair, E. Ross, 93
AFL-CIO, 83
Agency for International Development
(AID), 45, 46, 48, 49, 50, 64,
68–73, 80, 82, 83, 178n.
  Administrator of, 81, 99
  missions of, 48
  see also, David E. Bell
Agricultural Act of 1961, 63
agricultural surpluses, 7
  see also, surpluses of agricultural
  commodities
agricultural policy of the United States,
1–24
  tools of, 7
  postwar trends of, 39–45
Agricultural Trade Development and
Assistance Act of 1954
  see also Public Law 480 and Food
  for Peace
agriculture
  mobilization of, 6–7
aggressor nations
  aid to, 28, 92–93, 100, 107, 114, 116,
  131
Aiken, George, 40, 87, 96, 97
Alaska, 73, 96, 181n.
Albert, Carl, 91
Allies, 27
American Farm Bureau Federation, 6,
  39, 40, 42, 84, 88
  see also, farm groups and interest
  groups
American farmer, the, 102
  in the West, 3–4
  in the South, 3
  in the Plains area, 3–4
  in the feed-deficit areas, 4
American Jewish Joint Distribution
  Committee, 176n.
American Mission to Greeks, 176n.
American Merchant Marine, 96
American National Interest, 81, 135,
  139
American National Red Cross, 176n.

American Relief for Poland, 176n.
Anderson, Clinton P., 181n.
Argentina, 73
Arkansas, 95, 181
Australia, 39, 73

Bartlett, E. L., 96, 181n.
Bauer, Elizabeth K., 172n.
Beale, W. T. M., 61
Belcher, 41, 135
Bell, David E., 75, 81, 82, 83, 86, 87
  see also, AID Administrator
Benedict, Murray, 171n., 172n.
Benson, Ezra Taft, 40, 58, 60
Boggs, J. Caleb, 85
Bolton Amendment, 93
Bolton, Oliver P., 92
Borgstrom, George, 174n.
Bow, Frank T., 90, 91
Brannan Plan, 5
Bureau of the Census, 181n.
Bureau of the Budget, 45, 50
Butz, Earl L., 59

California, 93
Canada, 39, 73
CARE, 176n.
  see also, voluntary agencies
Cargo Preference Act, 86, 96
Castro's Cuba, 94, 135
  see also, Communist countries
Catholic Relief Service, 176n.
  see also, voluntary agencies
Cepede, Michel, 174n.
Chamber of Commerce, 83
Chairman of the House Committee on
  Agriculture, 99, 132
  see also, Harold D. Cooley
Chairman of Senate Committee on
  Agriculture and Forestry, 99,
  132
  see also, Allen J. Ellender
Chenery, Hollis B., 173n.
chi square analysis
  of Congressional respondents, 120–
  126

187